Also by Steven Key Meyers

Novels

My Hollywood Memoir and Other Fiction
(includes *Sidestep, Big Luck* and *Save the Max Man!*)

That's My Story
(plus *The Last Posse*)

Family Romance

My Mad Russian: Three Tales
(includes *Another's Fool* and *I Remember Caramoor*)

The Wedding on Big Bone Hill
(plus *Junkie, Indiana*)

Springtime in Siena
(plus *The Man Who Owned New York*)

All That Money

Good People

Plays

*A Journal of the Plague Year,
and Other Plays and Adaptations*
(includes *Chesterfield to His Son*)

Nonfiction

*The Man in the Balloon:
Harvey Joiner's Wondrous 1877*

THE MIDHURST LASHES

A screenplay adapted from
A.C. Swinburne's novels

Steven Key Meyers

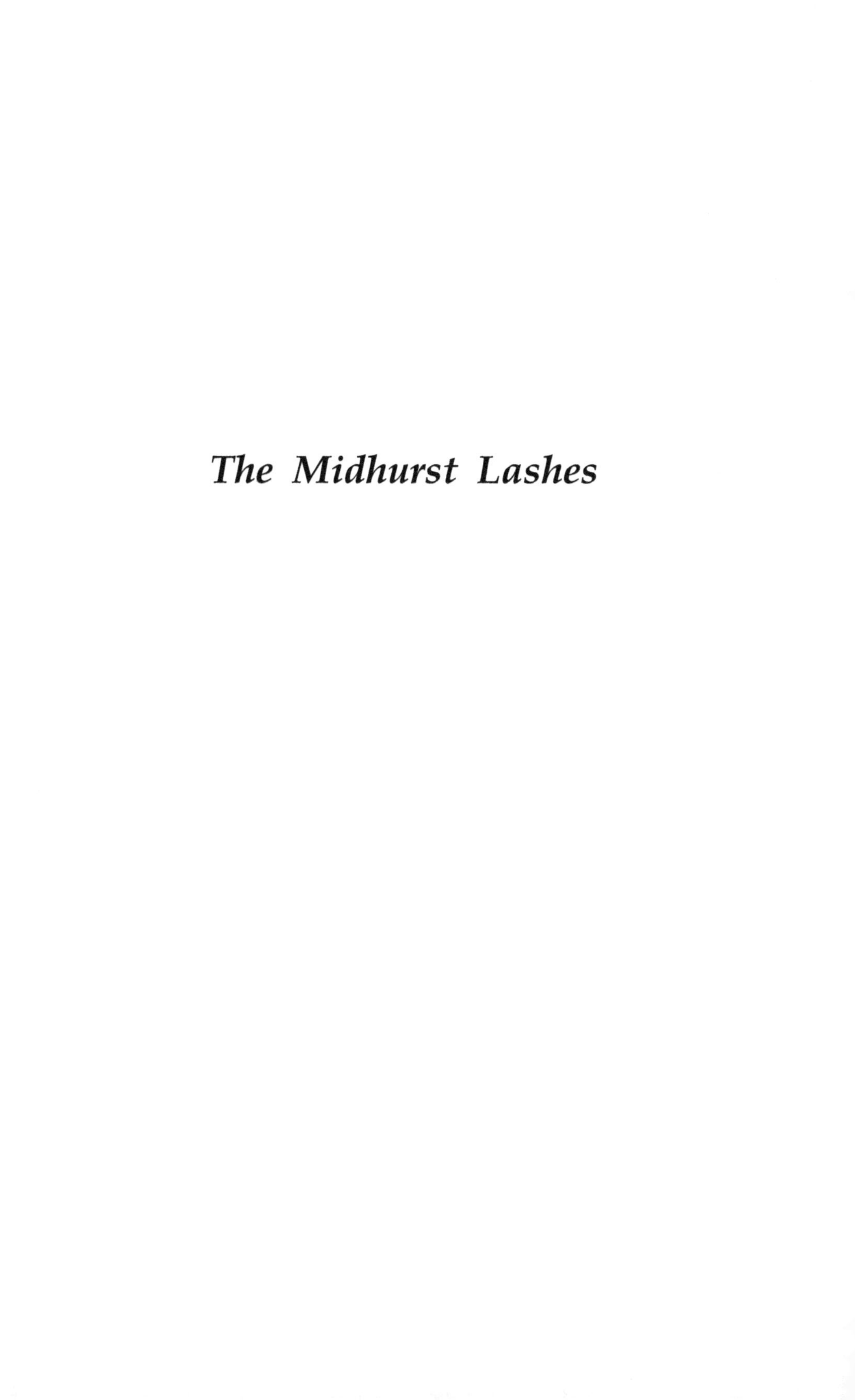

The Midhurst Lashes

for my first reader,
Albert F. Pesant
(1960 – 2023)

Contents

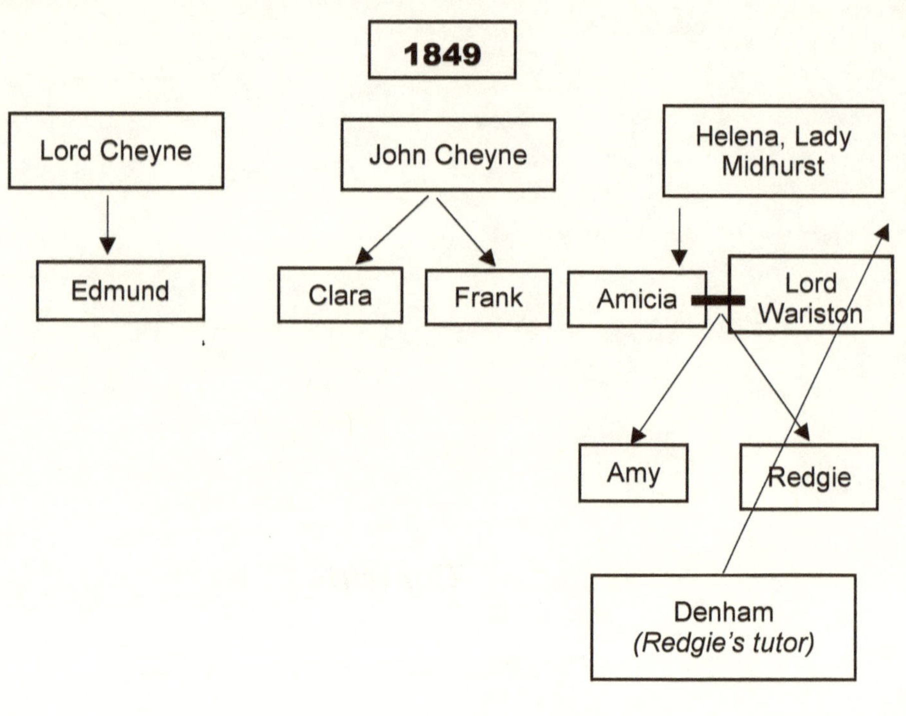

1849
Lord Cheyne
John Cheyne
Helena, Lady Midhurst
Edmund
Clara
Frank
Amicia
Lord Wariston
Amy
Redgie
Denham
(Redgie's tutor)

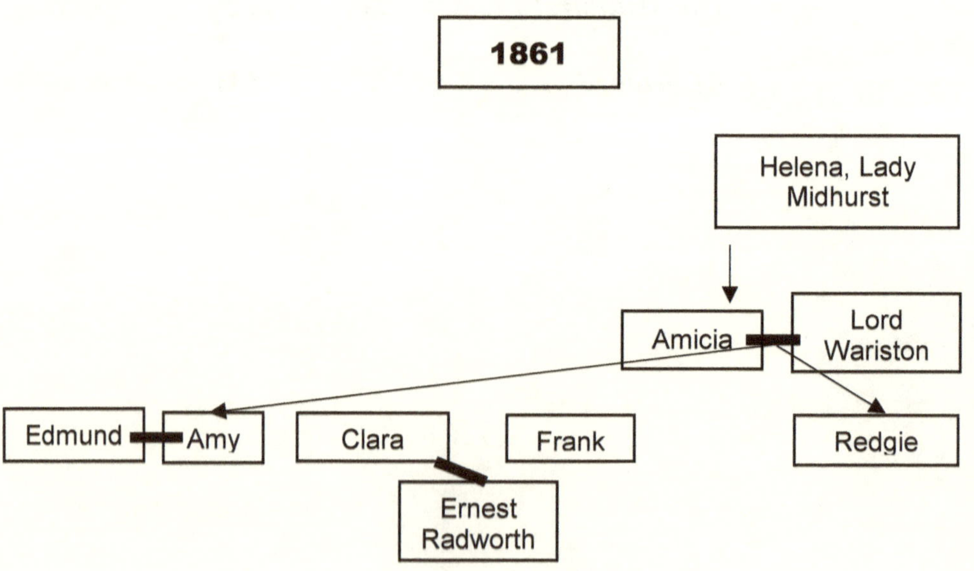

1861
Helena, Lady Midhurst
Amicia
Lord Wariston
Edmund
Amy
Clara
Frank
Redgie
Ernest Radworth

CAST OF PRINCIPAL CHARACTERS

1849

HELENA, LADY MIDHURST, 50
Her daughter, AMICIA, LADY WARISTON, 33
Amicia's husband, LORD WARISTON, 37
Their son, REDGIE SEYTON, 13
Their daughter, AMY SEYTON, 14
Redgie's tutor, DENHAM, 30
JOHN CHEYNE, 53, brother of Midhurst and Lord Cheyne
His son, FRANK CHEYNE, 10
His daughter, CLARA CHEYNE, 14
EDMUND CHEYNE, 14, son and heir to Lord Cheyne

1861

HELENA, LADY MIDHURST, 62
AMICIA, LADY WARISTON, 44
LORD WARISTON, 49
REDGIE SEYTON, 24
AMY, LADY CHEYNE, 26
Amy's husband, EDMUND, LORD CHEYNE, 26
CLARA CHEYNE RADWORTH, 26
Clara's husband, ERNEST RADWORTH, 41
FRANK CHEYNE, 22
ARMANDE DE ROCHELAURIER, 55
Her daughter, PHILOMENE DE ROCHELAURIER, 17

FADE IN:

A wild sea. REDGIE SEYTON appears on the stony shore. A wiry 13, he has long-lashed hazel eyes and dark gold hair.

TITLE:

Northumberland

1849

Redgie sees a boat caught in the surf with a terrified 10-year-old boy aboard. It vanishes, then rises empty on a wave. Redgie strips and leaps into the water. Breakers knock him down but he works his way beyond them to where high waves are piling up on the boy.

V.O.

Dear Mr. Swinburne: I have read your manuscript, and regret that I cannot pass upon it a favorable verdict. Apparently your sojourn in France has vitiated your principles and confused your judgment, for you bring upon the stage at least one married Englishwoman who prefers to her husband another man. This may happen on the Continent. Here it cannot happen.

It appears to me, sir, doubtful whether you have any sense of moral beauty. Morality is the soul of art. A story must be judged by the lesson it conveys. If it strengthens our hold upon fact, heightens our love of truth, rekindles our ardor for the right, it is good. If not, what shall we say of it? I remain yours sincerely.

Reaching YOUNG MATHISON, Redgie clutches at him, and a wave sweeps them both on shore. Redgie, cut and bleeding, chokes trying to catch his breath.

> REDGIE
> Here, fellow, get up. Stop shamming.
> (no response. Pulls Young Mathison
> farther up.)
> Won't you catch it for smashing your governor's boat. You are all right, aren't you? Aren't you?

Mathison snorts and chokes and sits up.

> REDGIE [cont'd]
> Knew you were shamming, little cad.

> YOUNG MATHISON
> If you hadn't come in, I'd have drowned! Drowned!

> REDGIE
> What a jolly lie! I didn't pull you out. Say I did and I'll punch your head.

> YOUNG MATHISON
> (offering hand)
> Sir, thank you—

                    REDGIE
Just you wait till I've got my breeches on,
I'll give you no end of a licking.

             YOUNG MATHISON
Thank you —

Stumbles off. Redgie laughs at the sea. He turns. DENHAM, his tutor, 30, stands astride Redgie's clothes, switching his legs with a stick. Tall and muscular, Denham has hard features and thinning dark hair.

                 DENHAM
Redgie, I told you not to bathe today.

                  REDGIE
Yes, Mr. Denham.

Denham grasps Redgie and whips him. Redgie, submitting, cries. Denham's face, contorted with effort, betrays a dawning satisfaction. From our angle the encounter looks sexual.

EXT. NORTHUMBERLAND MOORS – DAY

A train moves through the open mid-September landscape.

INT. TRAIN COMPARTMENT – DAY

HELENA, LADY MIDHURST sits beside a CURATE opposite her brother, JOHN CHEYNE. Midhurst is a beauty of 50, raven-haired, her face alight with intelligence. In dress she makes no concession to age. John Cheyne, 53, is the gross ruin of a handsome man. Cheyne and the curate read newspapers, Cheyne snapping his pages. Midhurst closes her French novel.

                    MIDHURST
Ashton Hildred is so pretty this time of
year.

                    CHEYNE
Dullest corner of England.

                    MIDHURST
I've sense enough still to enjoy the sight of
beauty. *Apropos,* my granddaughter visited
me last month: She promises to be a pure
beauty. And she has the Midhurst lashes.

She smiles at the curate.

                    CHEYNE
Never seen pure beauty. You must go into
heaven — or hovels — to find it.
    (smiles at curate)
The mother ages prettily, I'm told.

                    MIDHURST
Amicia is more beautiful than ever.

                    CHEYNE
They say it's a pity her hair will take no
sort of dye, for of course she has given it
the chance.

                    MIDHURST
Dark hair could not improve her. And her
eyes! One must go to Balzac to see such
eyes.

CHEYNE
She must have her followers then, as the
servants say. The husband's still a laboring
man?

MIDHURST
Lord Wariston lives on his own land.

CHEYNE
And does the son inherit the taste for farm
produce?

MIDHURST
Redgie's to be a cavalry officer — or a poet.

CHEYNE
Better the whip in his hand than a pen!
    (whips seat with newspaper;
    curate jumps)
I gave Denham to them, you know. He
might make something of any boy. Eager
to see how he's getting on.
    (to curate, from behind paper)
We spoil boys, sir — forget they must grow
up to be men. My motto is strike hard.
Nothing that bruises, mind: Black and blue
is hideous. But sting your victim well at
each cut.

MIDHURST
    (whispering:)
I apologize: My brother's notion of talk is
monologue plus a listener. Fortunately for
a younger son, he made a profitable union

in the bonds of unholy matrimony. Against her fortune, scandal never threw a word of suspicion. Her dearest enemy could not call her *poor*. Her friends had called her worse.
    (curate seeks refuge in his
    newspaper)
And your young things?

CHEYNE
Arrive tomorrow. My daughter—

MIDHURST
Our brother brings the unfortunate heir to the title.

CHEYNE
To think the next Lord Cheyne's another philanthropic idiot!

MIDHURST
Even so, cousins should know one another.

CHEYNE
So you brought this gathering about, eh?

MIDHURST
Oh do look at the gulls.

EXT. STATION NEAR ASHTON HILDRED – DAY

Midhurst and Cheyne transfer to a coach. Midhurst's maid JULIE and CHEYNE's MAN emerge, advanced in amorous talk. Midhurst directs her maid with a quiet "Julie!" The coach starts across the moors, servants necking on the roof.

EXT. FORECOURT OF ASHTON HILDRED – DAY

The coach arrives at Ashton Hildred, a stately old house looming above its park and the moors. On the other side it overlooks the sea.

TITLE:

Ashton Hildred

AMICIA, LADY WARISTON, Midhurst's daughter, a beautiful (if graying) 33, comes out.

CHEYNE
Lovely! Dear sister, my epigrams curl up at
sight of her and sting themselves to death.

MIDHURST
Dear Amicia!

AMICIA
(embracing them)
Mother! Uncle John!

They go inside. Julie and Cheyne's man move off, superintending house servants and kissing.

DISSOLVE TO:

EXT. SAME – NIGHT

Several hours later, we see through drawing room windows a party assembling before dinner. LORD WARISTON (Amicia's husband, 37, a hearty country squire) stands with Amicia, Midhurst, Cheyne, Denham and NEIGHBORS: CHALFORDS and FIELDFARES.

Redgie sits apart, next to his sister AMY, 14.

INT. DRAWING ROOM, ASHTON HILDRED – NIGHT

CLOSE-UP on Amy's eyes as she placidly watches the room's commotion. We see her pupils, then—pulling back—her clear golden irises, long lashes, dark eyebrows that meet, strong features and masses of golden hair.

The CAMERA, pulling back, takes in Redgie squirming at her side, then advances on his face. The relentless slow CLOSE-UP emphasizes their likeness, his coloring darker but his expression giving as little away.

Meanwhile, disconnectedly:

> FIRST MAN (O.S.)
> A blasphemous book, more offensive than
> I could have believed.

> FIRST WOMAN (O.S.)
> The work of a most apostolic man, the
> Reverend Swallow.

> SECOND WOMAN (O.S.)
> A man of that name was chaplain to Lord
> Sidmouth and tutor to the boy.

> SECOND MAN (O.S.)
> —and ended by robbing him of life as well
> as honor in a way too repulsive to think of.

> THIRD WOMAN (O.S.)
> That was Robert. His influence with young
> men was wonderful.

SECOND WOMAN (O.S.)
I don't believe it's natural, my dear.

THIRD WOMAN (O.S.)
Oh: metallic, serpentine, sick, musical and
poisonous. I quite see.

Wariston stands at a loss with Midhurst and Cheyne.

WARISTON
Amicia, where's Redgie? Your mother
hasn't seen him yet.
        (Redgie comes forward)
This is my son, Lady Midhurst.

CHEYNE
Pardieu! Where are his wings?

MIDHURST
I never saw such a beautiful young male.
Spoilt a good deal, I suspect.

WARISTON
Ask his tutor. Mr. Denham is responsible.

Midhurst gives Denham a hard look. He bows.

MIDHURST
And looks as if he knows it.
        (to Cheyne)
So that's your Denham. No, I recant: A
boy's not likely to get spoilt in such hands.

Denham comes up as Cheyne chucks Redgie under the chin.

CHEYNE
Well, sir, do they call you a good boy?

REDGIE
Not to my face.

CHEYNE
(to Denham)
Daresay he wants a brushing pretty often, to tickle the flies off? A little gentle irritation? A boy not worth his birch must be a blockhead or a blackguard.

DENHAM
He's quick enough, but infamous at arithmetic, and his verses are good once in two years.

CHEYNE
Flog him well when you do flog him. He will be grateful to you. Severity can do little for the boy — Indulgence, nothing.

WARISTON
Cheyne, if you will bring in Lady Midhurst.

Cheyne offers his arm to Midhurst. She hesitates.

MIDHURST
Tell me something, on your word of honor.

CHEYNE
Dear sister!

MIDHURST
I am aware that you employed Mr.
Denham before he came here. I'm also
aware of certain rumors. I'm sorry to have
to ask whether Mr. Denham is your natural
son?

CHEYNE
Oh Helena. Oh Helena. On my word of
honor: He is no connection of *mine*.

Midhurst looks at Denham — whispering intensely to Amicia —
and at Wariston, laughing with a neighbor.

MIDHURST
Good. He might have found his place
here — complicated.

By couples, all pass out of the drawing room.

INT. DINING ROOM OF ASHTON HILDRED - NIGHT

Redgie sits between Cheyne and MISS CHALFORD, 19. A
swarm of servants attends the table. Redgie eats his asparagus
by throwing back his head and dropping each spear down his
throat. Miss Chalford snubs her admirer on her other side
(YOUNG FIELDFARE, 19) by talking to Redgie.

MISS CHALFORD
My brothers shoot. Do you shoot? So
horrid. Dead creatures every day. I hear
you like the water: So unsafe. My brothers
never bathe. Do you like school? Oh yes,
you have Mr. Denham. How nice to have a

tutor. My brothers do go on about their
whippings at school.
>   (looks at Denham, who watches
>   Amicia)
Are you afraid of Mr. Denham?

REDGIE

No.

MISS CHALFORD

I'm afraid of men who look clever.
Mr. Denham looks—clever.

Young Fieldfare suddenly realizes why Redgie squirms. He
laughs. Miss Chalford looks from one to the other, puzzled.
Cheyne turns to Redgie.

CHEYNE

They tell me you write verse. Never could,
myself. Elegiacs! Forty years ago I was
always getting swished for my elegiacs!
>   (drops voice, nodding at
>   Midhurst)
In 1810 or thereabouts poor Tom Midhurst
and I were so used to our flogging every
afternoon we would toss up who should
go first. Plucky fellow, your grandfather.

Redgie looks at Midhurst, who speaks to SIR JOHN
FIELDFARE.

REDGIE

I should think he was.

CHEYNE
No chance of your coming in for such fare.
They spoil boys now. My motto —
  (drinks wine)
We were rather fast, I'm afraid — made
friends with our time. Midhurst ran wild
till he married my sister. Perhaps
afterwards, I don't say. She was
magnificent, I can tell you.

REDGIE
Was she really a stunner?

CHEYNE
She had rivals, and it was a famous time
for beauties — beauties long in the shank,
with flying manes, mouths that resisted bit
and bridle — but my sister won by long
odds.

They look at her.

MIDHURST
But you must then *pounce*, Sir John: *Pounce!*

A BUTLER whispers to Wariston, who takes his haunch of
meat out to where OLD MATHISON waits with Young
Mathison. As Wariston gnaws, his dogs crowding up, Old
Mathison talks. Meanwhile, disconnectedly from the table:

FIRST MAN (O.S.)
His work among those poor women has
indeed been blessed. One poor creature
said she couldn't believe one man could do
what he does among so many.

FIRST WOMAN (O.S.)
His wife heard of him at the public house
and went up to find him—

SECOND WOMAN (O.S.)
*—la tête reversée dans les seins de Cécile, qui
haletait comme une moribonde—*

THIRD WOMAN (O.S.)
But what made his neck yellow?

SECOND MAN (O.S.)
The way he sat Nicette. No boy could
handle her.

FIRST MAN (O.S.)
Mais mon Dieu, ça me paraît un peu bien fort.

SECOND WOMAN (O.S.)
Que veux-tu? C'est un genre.

FIRST MAN (O.S.)
De cannibale?

THIRD MAN (O.S.)
The golden age of topknots is over.

Wariston returns, beaming at Redgie. Redgie smarts.

MISS CHALFORD
(to Cheyne)
Your nephew's so handsome. Fancy the
rows he'll have with women.

CHEYNE
No, no: His is not the beauty which
endures, however pleasant while it lasts.

YOUNG CHALFORD
What's the use of good looks if they don't
last until they can help him to some fun?

CHEYNE
To give pleasure to others, as a song-bird
does, or a flower. You don't ask a rosebud
to turn into an apple. A deer does not
enjoy venison.

YOUNG CHALFORD
(to Young Fieldfare)
What the devil does that mean?

YOUNG FIELDFARE
Mad.

WARISTON
−so my son held on till the sea threw both
up together. A man could have done no
more.
(to Redgie)
Gallantly done, sir: gallantly done.

Murmurs of praise and ironic applause. Redgie blushes.

REDGIE
Please don't, you know I didn't really.

CHEYNE
Well done, my boy. Something to tell your
schoolfellows.

REDGIE
Oh please, look here, upon my word, I
funked. It makes a fellow feel a snake to
say I did when I didn't. Because I haven't
the pluck.

MIDHURST
Tears of the young Achilles.

CHEYNE
Cupid and the bee, rather.

Rising, Amicia leads the women out. Midhurst comes to
Redgie.

MIDHURST
Come with me. Your uncle's talk across the
wine pays no respect to the possible
innocence of boys.

Redgie goes out with her. The men crowding together,
Wariston passes wine.

OLD CHALFORD
Your sister wears well.

CHEYNE
Bah! Nothing now but husk and fangs.

WARISTON
Come, she's not a bad woman for a cynic.
I've been in love with her since I was
fourteen.

CHEYNE
She liked you back.
    (turns away from Wariston)
She always went in for innocence. Else
when she tired of Captain Harewood, *he*
would have married the daughter. Not that
she didn't propose him, but good
heavens—

DENHAM
Mr. Cheyne, the wine stands with you.

Cheyne fills his glass and pushes the bottle on.

CHEYNE
My brother also had a taste for lamb, but
no discernment. Tomorrow we see him
and his ass of a son. His wife— Wariston,
do you recall what Savigny said of the late
Lady Cheyne? He would talk as if every
woman were professional: *Peu de taille, pas
de maintien; mais des tours d'oeil, des jeux de
visage — et puis des jaimes!*

With dismay Sir John sees his son's eyes kindle.

SIR JOHN FIELDFARE
Lord Wariston, what are we to think of the
crops?

                    CHEYNE
*Elle avait une saveur plus femme que les autres
femmes. Personne ne jetait comme elle cette
odeur d'amour qu'on aspire avec ses nerfes, et
que même au loin fait frémir les narines de
plaisir.*

                    WARISTON
Pardon, Cheyne, but perhaps we sail a bit
too — erm —

                    DENHAM
          (to himself)
     Entre deux vins.

Cheyne drinks.

INT. DRAWING ROOM, ASHTON HILDRED – NIGHT

Midhurst, her face softened with kindness, sits by the fire with
Redgie. From the piano, Amy sings Swinburne's ballad *A
Jacobite's Farewell* beneath their conversation:

                    (AMY
*(There's nae mair lands to tyne, my dear,
And nae mair lives to gie;
Though a man think sair to live nae mair,
There's but one time to die.*

*(For a' things come and a' days gone,
What needs ye rive your hair?
But kiss me till the morn's morrow,
Then I'll kiss ye nae mair.*

(O lands are lost and life's losing,
And what were they to gie?
Fu' mony a man gives all he can,
But nae man else gives ye.

(Our king wons ower the sea's water,
And I in prison sair;
But I'll win out the morn's morrow,
And ye'll see me nae mair.)

MIDHURST
Will you tell me the truth about this?

REDGIE
I did go in after the kid, but when the
water bumped us together I thought he'd
drown us both, and I funked it, but then
the water threw us out.

MIDHURST
I am sorry it was brought up in that way.
Some boys would like the tribute. You
don't. But don't show it: You'll never get
through a crowd of fellows with such a
weight of nervousness. Don't be sensitive:
Leave that to dowagers and cats.

REDGIE
I like cats.

MIDHURST
So do I, but if you shed sparks when your
fur's rubbed backwards, there won't lack
hands to do it. With all the daring in the
world, you can't have manliness without

sense. Child, what odd eyes you have! Like sea water with sparkles of sunshine. How do you get on with that tutor?

REDGIE

I hate him.

MIDHURST

I needn't ask if he flogs you. Don't color and shuffle. Flogging never did a boy of 13 any harm.

REDGIE

I shall be 14 in early spring.

MIDHURST

As it's now early autumn, I don't see your point. I won't torment you. Don't stay if you hate old women.

Redgie nestles against her.

MIDHURST [cont'd]

Did you know our Jacobite ancestor made this song the night before his execution? I knew your father at your age. He took to me rather.

REDGIE

He is a stunning good fellow, only —

MIDHURST

— he should observe time and place? His intention was kind.

REDGIE
But Uncle John.

MIDHURST
Oh, Uncle John. Don't get any notion of
providential justice into your head. It
doesn't pay — except in the Bible, of course.

The men come in. Cheeks quivering, Cheyne watches Redgie
exchange a look with Amy. Denham sits and, fingers working a
pillow, compares the faces of mother, grandmother, daughter
and son.

Amy comes up.

MIDHURST
What a state you've sung this boy into!
There's a pulse beating in these fingertips.
  (to Redgie)
Wouldn't you like to head a forlorn hope
at this moment? There, go talk to Miss
Whatsit. She's to cool you down.

CHEYNE
Come here, boy. I want to ask you some
questions.

Redgie goes to him.

MIDHURST
  (to Amy)
Knowing one or two will hurt.

CHEYNE

Being a hero, of course you will speak
truth. I want to know when you were last
flogged?
(pounds Redgie's shoulder)
Come, you've tasted the twigs, haven't
you? With the fresh hard buds on? They
sting, don't they?

REDGIE

Sometimes.

CHEYNE

I thought so! And when did Denham last
make rhymes between his birch and your
body?

Redgie quivers with shame. Denham comes up.

REDGIE

This afternoon.

CHEYNE

I could have sworn it! Good heavens,
Denham, what a flogging you've given this
boy!

DENHAM

How can you see?

CHEYNE

As easily as if I saw him bathing! Don't
cry.

REDGIE
I'm not going.

Amicia flies over to comfort Redgie.

AMICIA
Oh dear! Today?

DENHAM
I saw he had bathed, my lady, against my
order. He said nothing of his deed.

CHEYNE
His little heroics. Flagrant injustice, eh,
boy? Delicious!

AMICIA
Poor child, if we'd known. I'm sure you
bore it well.

REDGIE
I blubbed like a girl. I'm a beastly coward.

CHEYNE
(to Denham)
If pain so beautifully subdues the boy's
face, I wager you're tempted to whip her,
too?

Denham turns fiercely away.

MIDHURST
Brother, when you have tormented the boy
enough will you come to my rescue?

Cheyne joins Midhurst, who releases Amy.

YOUNG FIELDFARE
(to Redgie)
Old chaps like to see a boy wriggle. But
you should have heard him over his wine.

REDGIE
I should like to wring his neck.

MIDHURST
(to Cheyne)
You've given him touch enough of the old
school.

CHEYNE
Lashed him to surpassing beauty. But his
bloom is brief. The girl—

MIDHURST
Amy?

CHEYNE
Amy will soon absorb his beauty: No law
of primogeniture for that.

MIDHURST
You think nature a democrat?

CHEYNE
By no means: Beauty is the exception and
exception means rebellion. People who go
in for beauty—poets and painters, men
who believe in life—are born aristocrats.
Given her way, nature would grow
nothing but turnips. Only the force that
fights her can rebel into a rose. In the long

run she beats us and we grow into wall-
fruit—old outside and in. The worst is that
some remember what they were like in
flower.

                    MIDHURST
The comfort is there will be flowers after
us to protest the turnips.

                 YOUNG FIELDFARE
Mr. Cheyne, did you ever write moral
essays?

                    MIDHURST
He thought of it once, but a friend
suggested adding a syllable to moral, and
of course he refrained.

INT. REDGIE'S BEDROOM – NIGHT

Redgie, half undressed, lets in Amy.

                      AMY
Lazy boy, you don't want me to sing you
to sleep.

                    REDGIE
Yes I do. I say, what a beastly time it's
been.

                      AMY
You get on with *grand-mère*. I used to be
her favorite.

REDGIE
She's a brick. But isn't Uncle John a brute!

AMY
Get into bed if you want to be sung to.

REDGIE
You sit there.

Pushing her into a chair, he kneels, holding one of her hands between his. She keeps time on his hair with her other hand as, looking into the fire, she sings Swinburne's *A Song for Margaret Midhurst.*

AMY
God send the sea sorrow,
And all men that sail thorough.
God give the wild sea woe,
And all ships that therein go.

My love went out with dawn's light;
He went down ere it was night.
Many sails went over sea;
One took my heart from me.

All they saving one
Came in landward under the sun.
Waves white and waves black,
One sail they sent not back.

Many maidens laughed that tide;
I fell down and sore sighed.
Many mouths I saw kiss;
No man kissed there mine, I wis.

I laid my head to the sea-stone;
I made my bed there alone.
Betwixen land and green sea
Swevens and sorrows fell on me.

I saw waves black and green,
But no man's sail between.
I found sorrow and much pain,
But not my love again.

God give me a green bed,
And no pillow to my head.
God give me brief life's breath,
And a good sleep after death.

REDGIE
You smell of flowers in a hot sun.

Redgie kisses her feet and her throat. Laughing, Amy kicks him away.

REDGIE [cont'd]
Oh tread me to death! Oh darling! It would be jolly to feel you killing me!

AMY
You are the most insane child I know. Now go to bed. Goodnight. I love you too. Let me go.

Dragging him to bed, she leaves. He falls asleep instantly.

EXT. SEA BELOW ASHTON HILDRED – DAY

A bright morning. Redgie and Denham swim. The waves beat Redgie up the shore but he plunges back in.

> DENHAM

Insatiable.

> REDGIE

Can't catch me!

Denham roars after him. Redgie, squealing, swims out. Denham comes up under him and lifts him high, both laughing.

EXT. SAME – DAY

Walking back, they meet Amicia. Redgie goes on ahead, turning around to watch as Denham and Amicia furtively touch at a turning of the path. Reaching the lawn, they see Midhurst on a bench, but turn away without acknowledging her. Looking grim, Midhurst beats her parasol on the ground.

INT. SCHOOLROOM, TOP OF ASHTON HILDRED – DAY

Denham, his desk piled with books, watches the sea dancing far below. Redgie has Homer's *Odyssey* open before him, but watches Denham.

> REDGIE

Sir, what was Circe like?

> DENHAM

Where do you find that question?

> REDGIE

No, but what do you think?

> DENHAM

I think Redgie Seyton will be flogged before long.

REDGIE
I want to know, please.

DENHAM
Look here, Redgie, if I have to flog you
again, you won't like it.

REDGIE
Have you noticed, sir, in every story, every
fight, there is a woman somewhere? I think
they were right to put women in the sea.
It's like a woman itself.

DENHAM
The way it lashes and caresses?

REDGIE
The right place for sirens to come out of
and sing and kill men.
     (points)
Look there, what a jolly wave for one to
come riding in upon.

DENHAM
They stay on shore now. But I don't know
they do the less harm for that.

REDGIE
Were the sirens really beautiful, or only
looked?

DENHAM
Ulysses would have gone in after them if
he could, and he was a hard man to take
in.

REDGIE
If he got Circe, how jolly for him.

DENHAM
He would have been happier than other
men. Or unhappier.

REDGIE
Is my mother as beautiful as Circe?

DENHAM
As Circe, and Calypso, and Penelope— I
will not be distracted! Go down, sir!

Unfastening his trousers, Redgie goes to the flogging block as
Denham chooses a birch. Midhurst enters.

MIDHURST
Oh my boy, I'm here to take you away
from this dangerous neighborhood. With
your pardon, Mr. Denham.

DENHAM
Your ladyship.

REDGIE
A holiday, *grand-mère?*

MIDHURST
Your cousins arrive soon and in their
honor we shall play proverbs. Go along,
there's much to do.

REDGIE
May I, sir?

DENHAM
Of course you may.

Redgie runs off.

MIDHURST
Mr. Denham, I am an old lady —

DENHAM
Not at all —

MIDHURST
An old lady who can see a man's face working with life repressed when desire curdles and he passes through quiet stages of perversion.

She kneads her parasol. Denham kneads the birch.

MIDHURST [cont'd]
But there are sins a man cannot act out and be rid of. These he must hold as though in his hand, clenching his fingers until his palm burns to the bone. My daughter, like the rest of us, has her role to play. I mean, of course, as regards the proverbs tonight.
    (looks at the sea)
How beautiful. The only sight of divine beauty in the world: A goddess, her cruelties and treacheries and subtle appetites part of her divine nature. . . You do my grandson a world of good, Mr. Denham. He is a small satisfied pagan.

DENHAM
Your ladyship?

MIDHURST
Like me.

Giving the sea a parting glance, she leaves.

INT. DRAWING ROOM OF ASHTON HILDRED – DAY

Furniture is pushed back and one end made into a stage.
Midhurst directs Amicia, Amy, Wariston, Redgie, Denham and
Cheyne in posing for a tableau. Cheyne disputes her directions.
We cannot quite follow the action or speech.

EXT. STATION NEAR ASHTON HILDRED – DAY

FRANK CHEYNE and CLARA CHEYNE, John Cheyne's son
and daughter, get off a train. Frank 10, is dark, small and shy.
Clara, 14, is blond, pretty and watchful. Clara prompts Frank to
inquire for Ashton Hildred's coachman, then prompts Frank to
have him secure their baggage. They climb into the coach.

INT. AMICIA'S SITTING ROOM – DAY

Servants help fit out the family in costumes. Midhurst wears a
yellow rococo dress, with a headdress rising to the ceiling.
Cheyne, in lacy blue silk and red heels, mimes taking snuff.
Wariston looks bewildered in black and yellow. TWO BOYS
are dressed as pages. Amicia is in white, Amy in orange,
Denham in crimson. Everyone rounds on Redgie.

REDGIE
Why can't I be a pageboy?

CHEYNE
Because we need another girl.

MIDHURST
Do behave, Redgie, or you'll spoil it.

They dress him in an orange dress like Amy's. Midhurst adds long hair to his, while Cheyne paints his face. Redgie glowers resentfully until, transformed, he begins a silent flirtation with the mirror's image of a pretty, delicate young lady.

CHEYNE
Quite passable.

MIDHURST
You're lovely, Redgie.

A coach rattles up to the house. Cries of "The coach!"

AMICIA
How am I to receive them? I can't go down
like this.

CHEYNE
Why not?

MIDHURST
And we might introduce—
(indicating Redgie)
your daughter. She is perfect.

CHEYNE
So is the suggestion: Perfect.

                    REDGIE
Not if I know it. Nuisance wearing this
beastliness.

                    MIDHURST
You won't ruin it and miss the best fun?

                    AMICIA
Do, Redgie. Be a good dog. I'll present you
as a rising poetess.

                    AMY
I'll sing you to sleep.

                    CHEYNE
              (to Redgie)
Keep that blush and the thing's done.

                    MIDHURST
              (to Cheyne)
If your son falls in love with her?

Cheyne looks furious.

INT. HALL OF ASHTON HILDRED – DAY

Frank is abashed as Cheyne leads the others in. Clara curtsies.

                    CHEYNE
Stand up straight, Frank. My daughter
Clara. My boy Frank. Lady Midhurst. Lord
and Lady Wariston, your cousin Amy—
and her sister Regina.

He pushes Redgie forward. Frank appears much struck.

CLARA
There's a boy in this house, I thought.

REDGIE
He's at school, the lazy brute.

MIDHURST
Her language! As her grandmother I ought
to look after it.

CHEYNE
Regina's a poetess.

CLARA
(inspecting Redgie's hand)
You look fonder of riding.

REDGIE
I like riding, too.

CLARA
How does your brother get on at school?

REDGIE
What a muff. Doesn't get swished half
often enough, I think.

MIDHURST
He keeps you well up to your slang, at any
rate.

CLARA
Is he older or younger?

A moment's hesitation.

                    REDGIE
Twin.

Everybody smiles.

                    CLARA
I should like to see him.

                    MIDHURST
When you've seen her you've seen him.

                    CLARA
He must be fond of you.

Redgie's grin changes to a girlish smile. Frank gives him his hand. Midhurst gleams with malice at Cheyne. Sound of another coach.

                    AMICIA
                  (nervously)
That must be Lord Cheyne.

EXT. FORECOURT OF ASHTON HILDRED – DAY

They walk out to a high coach, at whose window a pale face looms. The door opens and an unprepossessing figure climbs down: EDMUND CHEYNE, 14, son and heir of Lord Cheyne. He switches his leg with a short whip.

                    CHEYNE
                  (to Midhurst)
Where's Lord Cheyne?

                    MIDHURST
No doubt detained by the titillations of charity.

WARISTON
Well! You must be Edmund.

EDMUND
Father apologizes: Last night a meeting of
the Ladies Society for the Propagation of
Contagious Disease, and today pressing
needs among the streetwalkers to attend
to. A near thing *I* was able to come: I am
missing the Society for the Suppression of
Anatomy.

MIDHURST
Behold a man who will suffer sleepless
nights at the wrongs of women.

CHEYNE
And deserve them.

They go indoors. Frank now follows Amy, not Redgie.

INT. GUNROOM AT ASHTON HILDRED – DAY

Wariston helps Cheyne choose a shotgun, while Denham and
Edmund stand by. Only Edmund is not in costume.

WARISTON
Denham, care to shoot?

DENHAM
No, thank you, my lord.

WARISTON
Eh? Too bad.

> (handing Cheyne a shotgun)
> Like this one?

                    EDMUND
          May I come?

Cheyne sights along barrel at Edmund.

                    CHEYNE
          What is it, Denham? Some Homer to
          construe? Penelope entertaining the suitors
          in her husband's absence, perhaps?

Denham leaves. Wariston hefts a gun. Cheyne mimes taking snuff and sneezes in earnest. Edmund's eyes widen.

EXT. STABLEYARD OF ASHTON HILDRED – DAY

Redgie, wearing Amy's riding outfit, and Clara, got up something like a boy in Redgie's, prepare to mount horses. Amy, Frank and Edmund (switching at his calves) look on. Beyond, Wariston and Cheyne walk out with BEATERS and GAMEKEEPERS.

                    EDMUND
          May I ride?

                    CLARA
          Yes.

                    REDGIE
          No!

Redgie helps Clara mount. From horseback Clara sees Denham kissing Amicia in the schoolroom window.

CLARA
How clear is your sea air!

Redgie looks up at her ecstatically. He mounts and they trot out. Amy walks away.

EDMUND
May I come with you?

AMY
No. I must practice.

She and Frank flee hand in hand from Edmund. He catches up. Frank turns to fight, allowing Amy to escape into the house. Frank and Edmund tumble over a hedged garden. The CAMERA lifts up from them and looks through a window, finding Amy practicing her curtsey before a pier glass, while we overhear Edmund and Frank.

EDMUND (O.S.)
I shall marry that girl. That Amy. You
watch if I don't.

FRANK (O.S.)
I won't let you. I hate you.

EDMUND (O.S.)
You mean your father hates my father. So
do I, but he can't stop me. When he dies I'll
be Lord Cheyne.

FRANK (O.S.)
He'll cut you off with a shilling.

EDMUND (O.S.)
No, he can't, the estate's entailed! Don't you know anything, little 'un? I say, how old are you?

FRANK (O.S.)
Ten.

EDMUND (O.S.)
Father says the aim of every acquaintance should be reciprocal amelioration. Don't you agree?

FRANK (O.S.)
(apprehensively)
I don't know.

EDMUND (O.S.)
I say, were you ever swished?

FRANK (O.S.)
Swished?

EDMUND (O.S.)
Birched.

FRANK (O.S.)
Do you mean *flogged?*

EDMUND (O.S.)
Well, flogged, if you like that better.

FRANK (O.S.)
(ashamed)
I never was flogged in my life.

> EDMUND (O.S.)
> Good—! God—!

> FRANK (O.S.)
> Were you?

> EDMUND (O.S.)
> You should have seen me yesterday. My father draws blood at the third cut. Won't you sing out the first time you catch it?

CAMERA looks down to see Edmund handing his whip to Frank.

> EDMUND [cont'd]
> Look here, give me a cut as hard as you can. I should like it. Do, there's a good fellow. Hit hard, mind.

Edmund bends. Frank, inspired, delivers a stinging blow. Edmund jumps and yells and rubs his rear.

> EDMUND [cont'd]
> Well done! No need to mention this, you know. I wanted you to see what you'll be in for.

He takes back his whip.

INT. PARLOR AT ASHTON HILDRED – DAY

Amy is still practicing her curtsey when Midhurst comes in.

> MIDHURST
> Your mother, child?

AMY
I don't know, *grand-mère*. The schoolroom?

MIDHURST
Of course. Dear, go pay some attention to
your cousin Edmund. He's shy.

AMY
Yes, *grand-mère*.

Midhurst goes out. Frank enters and by way of adoration
dances a sort of jig before the pier glass.

FRANK
What are you doing?

AMY
What are *you* doing? Go away.

FRANK
But you are so beautiful!

Amy is reconciled.

INT. STAIRCASE OF ASHTON HILDRED – DAY
Midhurst walks grimly upstairs.

EXT. MOORS NEAR ASHTON HILDRED – DAY
Redgie and Clara are riding (both astride).

REDGIE
I say, do you write verses?

CLARA

People who write verses are bad, or mad, or sick.

REDGIE

It is odd how words change by being tied up and twisted back into rhyme. They get teeth and bite. Verse hurts horribly.

CLARA

One can't tell where the pain ends or the pleasure begins.

Redgie looks at her as though she is a prophetess.

CLARA [cont'd]

A woman's art is to marry.

REDGIE

Marry my brother. He would love you.

CLARA

Is he really like you?

REDGIE

The spit. No end good looking.

CLARA

I think you're plain. Shall I marry Edmund and become Lady Cheyne?

REDGIE

Marry — *him?*

CLARA
I don't think your grandmother would
enjoy calling me Lady Cheyne, do you?
But I must marry well. I want to be happy.

They reach a cliff overlooking the sea.

REDGIE
I wonder what dying's like. I feel one need
never die if one chose not. People do
choose, some time or other, and it's
remembered against them. You want to get
off dying, and the destinies remind you
once you prayed for death. If only one
could keep one's will strung up so as never
to—

CLARA
You don't make sense.

REDGIE
Look at the sea: No sense in that, and by
Jove, is there anything like it? Let's gallop.

They gallop past Wariston and Cheyne. Cheyne mimes taking
snuff. The beaters scratch their heads.

EXT. PARK OF ASHTON HILDRED – DUSK

Midhurst walks with a subdued-looking Amicia behind
Edmund and a reluctant Amy. Wariston and Cheyne return,
gamekeepers bearing their game. Redgie and Clara trot into the
stableyard.

INT. SMOKING ROOM OF ASHTON HILDRED – NIGHT

Midhurst brings Cheyne in and closes the door.

> MIDHURST
> I will be put off no longer.

> CHEYNE
> But surely your daughter takes her wifely
> duties seriously?

> MIDHURST
> These things have been known to happen.

> CHEYNE
> If so— Dear, dear.
>   (he rings, then lights a cigar)
> I'll have a word. Forthwith.
>   (a servant enters)
> Mr. Denham.

The servant withdraws.

> MIDHURST
> To prevent scandal you must take him
> back as your librarian.

> CHEYNE
> Oh sister, if only it were so simple—

> MIDHURST
> What don't I know?

> CHEYNE
> If your suspicions are true! We must bear it
> as best we can.

Denham enters.

> CHEYNE [cont'd]
> Ah, Denham.

> DENHAM
> Lady Midhurst. Sir.

> CHEYNE
> We wish to have a word. Regarding your
> relations with Lady Wariston. These things
> do happen, as my sister reminds me. I
> hope it's not a matter of *l'amour, l'amour,
> l'amour?*

> DENHAM
> With us it's all mixed up. I think she rather
> hates me. I don't want her to love me. I
> want her not to hate me, but to fear, and to
> give way.

> MIDHURST
> Mr. Denham, of course you can stay in this
> house no longer. Fortunately, Mr. Cheyne
> wants a librarian.

Cheyne raises a restraining hand.

> CHEYNE
> (to Denham)
> You must be told. Always meant you
> should know some day. People do me the
> honor to imagine— Never mind. But you
> are not legitimate.

DENHAM
(angrily)
I know that.

CHEYNE
Your father was my late brother-in-law, Sir
Thomas Midhurst.

Midhurst is as shocked as Denham. To Midhurst:

CHEYNE [cont'd]
Didn't you know? Tom saw to it he was
educated, able to make his own way.
(to Denham)
There's the material about you of a bad
novel and a good comedy.

Denham walks out slowly.

MIDHURST
Brother and sister! You may be fenced
against feeling, but you cannot be happy at
heart.

CHEYNE
As his guardian: heartbroken. But as a
Christian, I am resigned.

MIDHURST
Is it so amusing to scourge me through
them?

CHEYNE
I never heard of such a thing.

Midhurst leaves. Cheyne laughs and laughs.

INT. CORRIDOR AT ASHTON HILDRED – NIGHT

Denham calls Amicia out of the drawing room crowded with family and neighbors. We can make out a few words only. They do not touch.

> DENHAM
> You see it comes to this: Honor.

> AMICIA
> Not the face, darling. Ah, not your face.

INT. DRAWING ROOM OF ASHTON HILDRED – NIGHT

To piano accompaniment the tableau begins. Denham stands at center, next to Redgie; Cheyne, crowding Redgie, holds Denham's extended left wrist; Amy is on Denham's other side, with Midhurst, Wariston and the pages grouped near by. Amicia stands apart, beneath the prop arch with a grating standing open and a lock marked "Peradventure." Amicia and Denham (the mute central figure) look at each other agonizedly throughout the tableau, whose lines are Swinburne's *A Cameo*.

> MIDHURST
> There was a graven image of Desire
>> Painted with red blood on a ground of gold
>> Passing between the young men and the old.

> REDGIE
> (curtseying)
> And by him Pain, whose body shone like fire.

> AMY
> (curtseying)
> And Pleasure with gaunt hands that grasped their
>> hire.

CHEYNE
Of his left wrist, with fingers clenched and cold,
The insatiable Satiety kept hold,
Walking with feet unshod that pashed the mire.

REDGIE
The senses and the sorrows and the sins,
And the strange loves that suck the breasts of Hate
Till lips and teeth bite in their sharp indenture,
Followed like beasts with flap of wings and fins.

AMICIA
Death stood aloof behind a gaping grate,
Upon whose lock was written *Peradventure*.

They hold the tableau while the pages open the grating and snuff out the lights. Applause.

DISSOLVE to:

INT. SAME – NIGHT

The guests are gone except for ERNEST RADWORTH, 29, heavy, graying and wearing thick lenses that focus on Clara. Wariston belches.

WARISTON
Amicia, will you play? My digestion.

MIDHURST
A treat for the children.

Amicia sits at the piano.

DENHAM
My lord, did you forget to lock the
gunroom?

WARISTON
Eh? Thanks, Denham.

Hands Denham a key. Denham goes out. Wariston naps.

AMICIA
It's called *The Weary Wedding.*

Amicia sings Swinburne's ballad with an emotion that makes
the cousins listen with wonder. Meanwhile Midhurst plucks
the false hair from Redgie's head and Redgie unconsciously
rubs off his paint. Clara watches his transformation,
astonished.

AMICIA [cont'd]
And what will you give for your father's love
One with another.
Fruits full few and thorns enough.
Mother, my mother.

And what will you give for your mother's sake?
One with another.
Tears to brew and tares to bake,
Mother, my mother.

And what will you give your sister Jean?
One with another.
A bier to build and a babe to wean,
Mother, my mother.

And what will you give your sister Nell?
One with another.

The end of life and beginning of hell,
Mother, my mother.

And what will you give your brother Ned?
One with another.

Gunshot O.S.

          AMICIA [cont'd]
Death for a pillow and hell for a bed,
Mother, my mother.

          WARISTON
     (waking up)
Poachers? Eh, what?

          AMICIA
And what will you give your sister Kate?
One with another.
Earth's door and hell's gate,
Mother, my mother.

And what will you give your brother Will?
One with another.
Life's grief and world's ill,
Mother, my mother.

And what will you give your brother Hugh?
One with another.
A bed of turf to turn into,
Mother, my mother.

And what will you give to your bridegroom?
One with another.

A barren bed and an empty room,
Mother, my mother.

The butler calls Wariston from the room.

AMICIA [cont'd]
And what will ye give your bridegroom's friend?
One with another.
A weary foot to the weary end,
Mother, my mother.

And what will ye give you your bridesmaid?
One with another.
Grief to sew and sorrow to braid,
Mother, my mother.

And what will you wear for your wedding
gown?
One with another.
Grass for the green and dust for the brown,
Mother, my –

Wariston comes in.

WARISTON
An accident.

Denham's bloody-breasted, crimson-clad dead body is carried past the door. Amicia faints. Wariston helps take her out. Cheyne watches with shining eyes.

CLARA
(to Redgie)
You're a boy! An ugly, ugly boy!

MIDHURST
Amy, you know the song?

Amy sits down at the piano and continues the ballad beneath the dialogue:

(AMY
(And what will you wear for your wedding lace?
One with another.
A heavy heart and a hidden face,
Mother, my mother.

(And what will you wear for your wedding ring?
One with another.
Weary thought for a weary thing.
Mother, my mother.

(Her tears made specks in the velvet and vair
One with another.
The seeds of the reeds made specks in her hair,
Mother, my mother.)

Clara turns to find herself reflected in Radworth's spectacles. She goes up to Edmund.

CLARA
Father says philanthropy is Greek for the love of men.

EDMUND
Philos, love. *Anthropos*, man.

CLARA
I do so wish to be a philanthropist.

She throws looks at Midhurst and Redgie.

DISSOLVE TO:

EXT. LIDCOMBE – NIGHT

The song continues. We dimly see, through falling snow, the façade of the grand Cheyne family seat.

TITLE:

Lidcombe

TITLE:

Eleven years, four months later.

TITLE:

1861

INT. LONG GALLERY AT LIDCOMBE – NIGHT

The song continues, Amy, Lady Cheyne (25 and married to Edmund, 25, who is now Lord Cheyne) playing and singing in her own drawing room. She, Edmund, Clara (25), Radworth (41, now Clara's husband), Redgie (24), Frank (21) and Midhurst (61) sit in the same relative positions as in the previous scene. Redgie has grown up vivid and poetic-looking, a male version of Amy, who is a willowy Pre-Raphaelite beauty. Frank is big, handsome and dark, much like Clara, except that she is blonde; her beauty hints of matronliness. Edmund and Radworth are homely and ungainly, Radworth entirely gray. Midhurst's white hair marks the sole change in her appearance. Redgie and Radworth watch Clara. Frank and Edmund watch Amy. Midhurst watches everyone.

AMY

He kissed her under the gold on her head,
One with another.
The lids of her eyes were like cold lead;
Mother, my mother.

He kissed her under her shoulder sweet,
One with another.
Her throat was weak, with little heat,
Mother, my mother.

He kissed her down by her breast-flowers red,
One with another.
They were like river-flowers dead,
Mother, my mother.

He kissed her under the fall of her chin,
One with another.
There was right little blood therein,
Mother, my mother.

What ails you now o' your weeping, wife?
One with another.
It ails me sair o' my very life,
Mother, my mother.

Nay, ye are mine while I have my breath:
One with another.
O fool, will you marry the dust of death?
Mother, my mother.

Yea, ye are mine, we are handfast wed,
One with another.

Nay, I am no man's; nay, I am dead,
Mother, my mother.

MIDHURST
Thank you, child.

EDMUND
Very pretty, my dear.

RADWORTH
Charming, Lady Cheyne, charming!

REDGIE
Amy, what on earth possessed you to play
that?

Redgie begins to walk up and down. Frank plays a four-handed waltz with Amy beneath the dialogue. Radworth and Edmund (carrying a riding crop) stroll up and down together. Midhurst is the center around which everyone orbits.

RADWORTH
So accomplished a wife ornaments your
leisure, Lord Cheyne.

EDMUND
As Clara does yours, Radworth — save that
leisure I have none. My time is given over
to emancipation, the right of voting, the
adulteration of food, morality, sewerage —

Redgie passes Midhurst and Clara.

CLARA
Redgie! Your grandmother's telling me
about an old novel called — *Vingt-et-Un?*

MIDHURST

Some such name—I know there are cards
in it. I am the Lady Manhurst of that book.
I break the heart of a rising poet. I make
two brothers fight a duel. I run off with
Lord Avery. I poison my husband. I hope I
finally enter the convent, but I forget.
      (Clara laughs.)
My friend Lady Wells wrote it. I had to
give her up in the long run.

You may take her as soon as I beg a favor
of her, Redgie.

Redgie resumes walking.

CLARA

Any service I might do, Aunt Helena.

MIDHURST

I want to see the family on comfortable
terms — especially to see you and Amy
friends.

CLARA

We *are* friends.

MIDHURST

There has been a coolness of late. You and
Edmund were so intimate before he
succeeded to the title that he must regret
this change, and Amy wants a companion.
Men have their uses, but you cannot live
on them.

CLARA
Of course I will be what I can to her.

MIDHURST
I rely on your head. Nothing but a good
clear head can get us through in quiet.

CLARA
Aunt, you mystify me.

MIDHURST
Your brother. You must have heard the
absurd rumors about Frank's last stay.
People talk of his devotion to poor Amy.
There can be nothing to it: He's hardly of
age, and besides, Edmund and Amy are
devoted to each other.

CLARA
Then what causes concern?

MIDHURST
Occupation suffices for him, but emotion is
wanting to her.

CLARA
Should you not speak to Frank yourself?

MIDHURST
A screeching old aunt, running round with
ruffled feathers? I have no intention of
helping people laugh at my white hair.

CLARA
It turned suddenly, didn't it?

MIDHURST
Your father's death was a shock. Both my
brothers are dead and my thoughts turn to
the young people. Your husband must be
such a support.

She nods to Radworth, strolling past with Edmund.

CLARA
Ernest has taken to bones.

MIDHURST
You would not have been happy with
Edmund.

CLARA
Perhaps a word to *him* about Frank—?

MIDHURST
La bonne farce! Edmund playing Othello?
No, a sister older and wiser is the best help
a boy can have to avoid scandal and the
light—rather, the twilight—of publicity.

CLARA
I expect hardly to see Frank, with Redgie
here. They are always together.

MIDHURST
Oh, Redgie. Be nice to him, my dear. He is
just now much "sat upon," as he puts it.

CLARA
His disgrace at Oxford—

MIDHURST
Lord Wariston behaves as if everyone
else's son saves up his allowance. No, it is
time for him to begin life. I don't mean
joining the bar or the Church.

Midhurst and Edmund exchange nods as he and Radworth
pass. Amy and Frank begin to walk up and down.

EDMUND
—the equilibrium of society, the
reformation of criminals and above all—

RADWORTH
Yes? Yes?

EDMUND
—the destiny of women.

MIDHURST
Poor man. Amy, my darling, come to me.

Amy and Frank come up.

CLARA
Amy, your music is ravishing.

MIDHURST
(to Clara, dismissively)
Thank you, dear.

Amy sits down. Clara goes off on Frank's arm.

CLARA
One always heard about her wit and
insight and power of reading character.

Her satire's vicious, but stupid and
pointless. Like looking at that old face and
remembering she was thought a beauty.

FRANK
What was she saying?

CLARA
Lady Midhurst thinks the household
harmony suffers from your presence.

FRANK
I don't understand.

CLARA
She tells me you think of falling in love
with limp little Amy.

FRANK
There should be a penal colony for old
women! It comes of the infamous reading
which the Midhurst must indulge in.

CLARA
There is a true side to that way of looking
at things.

FRANK
I never can believe that she helped bring
up Amy. She left nothing of her mark on
her.

Passing Midhurst and Amy, they smile and nod.

CLARA
Do you like her brother?

FRANK
His admiration of *you* is immense. You see,
mention Amy and I shall retort with the
desirable Redgie.

Edmund and Radworth pass.

EDMUND
The appetite for doing good gains in vigor
with advancing years—unlike baser
appetites, which time effaces and
enjoyment allays.

RADWORTH
A cheering truth.

They nod to Midhurst.

MIDHURST
(to Amy)
We lived apart the last ten years of his life.
Odd he should take it to heart. When I saw
him last he was grayer than Ernest
Radworth. That wife of his: enough to turn
any man gray—Ernest's, I mean. She'll be
the ruin of poor Redgie if we don't keep
him out of her way.

AMY
You suggested we have him here with
them.

MIDHURST

I did, thinking you would do the reverse of what an old woman told you. Here is my advice. Construe it by contraries: Keep Frank beside you, encourage Clara and be the fool with your husband.

AMY

Edmund and Clara—?

MIDHURST

There is your game.

AMY

When I remember how she courted him, I am uneasy.

MIDHURST

She cares more just now for the younger bird. (I declare, the woman makes me talk her style.) If you hold her off Redgie, I warrant your husband against her.

AMY

I thought you had me ask them because you knew I wanted Frank here—

MIDHURST

—and Clara makes a firescreen for you? I am not so liberal as that. But Frank is a nice boy. Go tell him I say so.

AMY

Yes, *grand-mère.*

Amy joins Clara and Frank as they pass. Midhurst signals
Redgie, who joins her though his eyes follow Clara.

> MIDHURST
> Redgie, Redgie: I should like to flog you. It
> is the only way to manage a dunce. The
> stinging of birch rods is nothing to the
> viper bites you run the risk of.

> REDGIE
> You cannot know the risk —

> MIDHURST
> I have been stung, and I have been talked
> of.

> REDGIE
> If you feel my presence a threat to Clara —

> MIDHURST
> You are no threat to Clara. Clara is the
> cleverest stupid woman I know, but
> nothing more. She can't be better than her
> style, but she won't be worse. The upshot
> is she's the safest woman alive. Not safe
> for her husband, mind — or for you. But as
> safe for herself as I am, or the Queen.

> REDGIE
> You don't think Ernest would rub his
> spectacles if — ?

> MIDHURST
> Ernest! She never was in love but once —
> with Edmund. You were at school. She

fought for the title with delicious dexterity, but his father wouldn't hear of cousins marrying. Her defeat steadied her for life, and she married Ernest in six months. When my brother died, I married Edmund to our little Amy. Don't worry, you goose: Amy knows all about it. No, the risk is to you.

Radworth (excited) and Edmund (bored) pass.

RADWORTH

—bones proving the range of motion was not—
(flaps his arms)
but rather—
(flaps arms wider)
The implication! To those who doubt me, I say come to Blocksham and see my bones!

REDGIE

How do you mean, steadied her?

MIDHURST

Cooled her down—made her sensible. At your age you cannot understand how anybody can be at once excitable and cold. She can enjoy herself, her excitability secures that. But she will never pay too high a price for anything. If she were more clever, she would be good training for you.

REDGIE

If she knew you spoke of her thus.

MIDHURST
(rising)
Tell her. I don't want my nice old Redgie sacrificed on a tinsel side-altar. I must be good to waste my time on girls and boys even younger than their ages. You should stick to dolls and cricket. Good night, Redgie. Good night, everybody, good night.

EDMUND
Good night, Lady Midhurst. Welcome to Lidcombe.

Midhurst goes out. Frank, Clara and Amy come up to Redgie. He looks glumly up at Clara.

FRANK
You look as though the Pope had stolen a march on Garibaldi.

CLARA
(to Redgie)
Your grandmother says I'm to be nice to you.

AMY
(to Frank)
Grand-mère warns me to be careful of you.

FRANK
And Clara warns me of you. Do let's keep watch on each other. Only then can we be safe.

Amy and Frank sink onto a settee. Clara sits down beside Redgie. Edmund and Radworth pass.

                    EDMUND
—public baths, reading rooms, and my
father's special concern: fallen women. My
father assisted I should think *hundreds* of
fallen women to make their living.

                    RADWORTH
Truly a gentleman.

EXT. FORECOURT OF LIDCOMBE – DAY

Two open carriages set out. In one, Amy and Clara face Frank
and Redgie. In the other, Midhurst faces Edmund and
Radworth.

EXT. MOORS NEAR LIDCOMBE – DAY

The carriages approach Hadrian's Wall. Edmund points his
whip.

                    EDMUND
There, Radworth: Hadrian's Wall.

                    RADWORTH
Oh yes?

                    MIDHURST
I perceive we approach from the barbarian
side.

                    RADWORTH
Redgie mentioned a temple—

> EDMUND
> As if modern religion were not cross
> enough, our deuced old Roman temple! I
> beg your pardon, Lady Midhurst.

She bows.

In the other carriage:

> REDGIE
> I have not made the pilgrimage for years.

> AMY
> A shrine?

> REDGIE
> A temple: A Mithraic temple, from Roman
> times.

EXT. ROMAN TEMPLE AT HADRIAN'S WALL – DAY

Redgie leads both parties on foot to a jumble of stones jutting
out: an ancient Roman temple sheltering a Mithraic bas-relief.
Redgie runs his hand over it.

> REDGIE
> The legions posted here were devoted.
> See? Their sacred image: Mithras, Protector
> of the Empire, cuts the bull's throat. And
> where his blood spurts new life grows.

Midhurst and Clara glitter. Amy turns away.

> CLARA
> Is Mithras a god?

                    REDGIE
God of a religion of power and blood.
Nothing invisible, nothing spiritual to it.
You see the slaughter and you accept it as
the only divine impulse this world knows
of.

                  MIDHURST
How appealing.

                    CLARA
Appalling, rather.

                     AMY
It's horrible!

                  EDMUND
Come, Amy, don't be so Christian!

Frank joins Amy in looking over the moors.

                    FRANK
I prefer the view, too.

                  EDMUND
I say, Radworth, yonder cottages have the
worst drains in the north of England!
Twice I've rebuilt them, but something in
the soil or the gradient defeats me.
     (low)
Near by, they tell me —

                  RADWORTH
Eh?

EDMUND
—thrives a two-headed calf!

RADWORTH
My word. Could we possibly—?

EDMUND
Let's. This is too dull.

EXT. MOORS NEAR LIDCOMBE – DAY

The carriage bearing Midhurst, Edmund and Radworth moves toward cottages.

EDMUND
Good of you, Lady Midhurst.

RADWORTH
I say, it is indeed.

MIDHURST
We are the elders. Let the young people enjoy themselves.

EXT. MOORS BELOW HADRIAN'S WALL – DAY

Redgie and Clara stroll below the temple.

CLARA
Am I being nice to you?

REDGIE
I should hope so, your own cousin who fell in love with you—and Mazzini—at thirteen.

CLARA

Do put Mazzini aside for a day.

REDGIE

I will, since you ask. But if he bade me I would follow him into hell.

CLARA

Not into hell!

REDGIE

One must do more than give one's poor little life. One must give one's honor.

CLARA

Redgie!

REDGIE

A gentleman must lie, and forge, commit murder, betray men and cut purses, if it would serve the cause.

CLARA

Reasoning with you is like talking to a conflagration.

REDGIE

Is it?

CLARA

Come, my conflagratory cousin, time to find the others.

He kisses her.

CLARA [cont'd]
You see, I am nice to you.

REDGIE
You are an angel to me.

Frank and Amy walk on the other side of Hadrian's Wall.

AMY
Ernest is so good for Clara. Scientific
pursuits must be the salvation of country
life.

FRANK
But your husband has his social aims. He
does much good, like his father before him.

AMY
Does he? He repels me, Frank.

Frank offers his arm.

AMY [cont'd]
I can't. I'm to be careful of you.

FRANK
And I of you, remember? When you are
out of my sight, who knows what you
might not do? But here with me, I know
nothing wrong goes on.

AMY
If we behave the same, each towards the
other —

FRANK
As in a mirror.

AMY
Then we are safe.

He kisses her.

EXT. VILLAGE ON THE MOORS – DAY

Edmund ecstatically mucks about a puddle. Midhurst and
Radworth sit bored in the carriage.

EDMUND
I say, these drains are blocked! I must dig
them up again!

EXT. MOORS BELOW HADRIAN'S WALL – DAY

Clara and Amy sit on a pile of stones. Frank and Redgie walk
uphill. They halt.

REDGIE
How do you like my Lord Cheyne? A faint
flavor of impertinence, I believe?

FRANK
Edmund was never *gracious* to me before.

REDGIE
You goose, as my grandmother would say.

FRANK
She worries me.

REDGIE
The Midhurst?

FRANK
Amy. She's lately nervous, with a way of
fretting her lip when her husband comes
in.

REDGIE
"When her husband comes in"? Oh Frank.
Scenes?

FRANK
Subdued, muffled-up scenes, is all.

REDGIE
Take care! Lest the friction of suspicion rub
the edge off his philanthropic eye.

FRANK
They say you resemble her, but I don't see
it. She is so very beautiful.
       (tracing Redgie's features with
       his hand)
Her eyebrows make the eyes effective and
soft, and her cheeks, perfect in form, have
the flush of a growing flower.

Redgie touches Frank's face.

REDGIE
Nor are you like Clara. Her nose is
straight, the shell of the nostrils exquisite
in cutting, and her brows take a rich curve
towards the temples.

INT. A BARN – DAY

Inside a barn Radworth fondles a two-headed calf. Edmund and Midhurst wait in the carriage.

> RADWORTH
> (calling:)
> I must have it — *them*, that is. The prize of my museum — *prizes*, I mean.

EXT. MOORS BELOW HADRIAN'S WALL – DAY

Amy and Clara wait on a slope.

> AMY
> It's raw here.

> CLARA
> Warm in the sun.

> AMY
> I don't like it. Too pagan.

> CLARA
> Your brother loves this sort of country.

> AMY
> Clara, I am glad you and Ernest came to stay with us. *Grand-mère* says he's a man of true provincial mark. I admire a man who chooses his field and works at it steadily.

> CLARA
> Edmund does that.

                    AMY
That's what I mean. We must be alike to
have married such men.

Clara stares.

                    AMY [cont'd]
Men so different from our brothers. Mine's
insane about politics. I don't mean
Edmund's, Redgie has no concern for
English politics: He burns over the fate of
peoples he has never seen.

                    CLARA
Absurd.

                    AMY
So I tell him: A waste of feeling.

                    CLARA
But better Italian enthusiasms than English
politics? Really?

                    AMY
My husband's gone through that stage and
become an ally, on principle, of strong
government.

Redgie and Frank approach from behind.

                    CLARA
Redgie tells me Edmund thinks of taking
his seat in the House of Lords and moving
you to London. Will you like being a
political hostess?

                    AMY
Oh no.

                   CLARA
You did not marry the title without
knowing what is incumbent upon its
holder's lady?

                    AMY
No. But my life lies more and more in the
private side to things.

                   CLARA
While your brother yearns to be — a
martyr?

                    AMY
I wish there were no *questions* in the world.

                  REDGIE
You prefer a man who turns over rocks
and disinters skeletons?

Kneeling, Redgie looks up adoringly at Clara. Amy gazes up
into Frank's eyes.

EXT. MOORS NEAR LIDCOMBE - DUSK

The carriages return home.

INT. LONG GALLERY AT LIDCOMBE - NIGHT

Midhurst, bored, sits between Edmund and Radworth. In a far
corner, Redgie and Clara sit absorbed; in another, Frank and
Amy.

> EDMUND
> —good men, but incapable of appreciating
> the equalization of society, the absolute
> republic or the forces of the future. Don't
> you agree, Lady Midhurst?

Midhurst's mouth opens and closes but no sound issues.

INT. CORRIDOR AT LIDCOMBE – DAY

Midhurst superintends Julie in assigning her trunks to
servants. She turns to Amy.

> MIDHURST
> I told Edmund I had a wire. I hope he
> doesn't question the kitchen: I lied.

> AMY
> Oh *grand-mère,* I feel bad—

> MIDHURST
> I'm not wanted here, and as I like to be the
> center of attention, I will be better off in
> London.

They set off in procession.

> AMY
> I hope you weren't bored.

> MIDHURST
> I assure you not! I have vastly enjoyed
> myself in catching up with all of you.

AMY

Oh *grand-mère,* you have no idea what I am feeling. Frank. . .

At the top of the staircase she begins to cry.

MIDHURST

Amy, married ladies cannot fail in their duties. Recollect that you are devoted to your husband and he to you. Any other hypothesis is impossible. As to being in love, I believe wine will intoxicate, rain will drench and fire singe — *not* that one person will fascinate another.

AMY

Oh *grand-mère.*

MIDHURST

Do not indulge in tragedy out of season.

AMY

Oh God, that one can yearn at heart to do or say what, if it were said or done, would strike one dead with shame!

Amy weeping hysterically, Midhurst embraces her.

MIDHURST

I wish the surgeons could amputate *sentiment.* I hate the very word. Sentiment is a mongrel breed between principle and impulse. Nothing is so dangerous: Not passion, not vice. To act on sentiment is ruinous.

(starts downstairs)
Oh child, come to London. Be moving. Get something done. Have done with the country.

EXT. MOORS NEAR LIDCOMBE – DAY

Clara gallops with Redgie, her hair blowing across his face. She pulls up.

REDGIE
You are the pluckiest rider I ever saw.

CLARA
I feel better now.

REDGIE
What kind of life does that monster leads you?

CLARA
People come to Blocksham with objects—stones and bones. Last week we received an ichthyologist—a man with pink eyes and a mouth on one side.

REDGIE
The swine! And you obliged to be civil!

CLARA
It has been nice here.

REDGIE
Stay. Or let me follow you and be your
footman, and clean knives and black boots
and see you constantly —

Clara gallops on, laughing. Redgie follows.

INT. LIBRARY AT LIDCOMBE – DAY

Frank reads to Amy from Swinburne's *Anactoria*.

FRANK
"My life is bitter with thy love; thine eyes
Blind me, thy tresses burn me, thy sharp sighs
Divide my flesh and spirit with soft sound.
I feel thy blood against my blood: my pain
Pains thee, and lips bruise lips, and vein stings
            vein.
Let fruit be crushed on fruit, let flower on flower,
Breast kindle breast, and either burn one hour —"

Edmund enters smiling and stands at the fire.

EDMUND
The servants said they heard you at
prayers. Do go on.

FRANK
"Ah that my lips were tuneless lips, but pressed
To the bruised blossom of thy scourged white
            breast!
Ah that my mouth for muses' milk were fed
On the sweet blood thy sweet small wounds had
            bled!
That with my tongue I felt them, and could taste

The faint flakes from thy bosom to the waist!"
Edmund goes out.

                    FRANK [cont'd]
          "That I could drink thy veins as wine, and eat
          Thy breasts like honey! That from face to feet
          Thy body were abolished and consumed,
          And in my flesh thy very flesh entombed!"

EXT. BELGRAVE SQUARE, LONDON – DAY
Trees are in leaf in front of Midhurst's house.

                    TITLE:

                    London

INT. MIDHURST'S DRAWING ROOM – DAY
Midhurst looks over manuscripts with Redgie.

                    MIDHURST
          I know one or two publishers. I shall pet
          them and wave these at them. Verse shall
          be your escape valve. Your *Ode to Mazzini*
          shall solder up your *téte fêlée*.

                    REDGIE
          Do as you wish. My verses are a part of
          me — but a dead part, cut off.

He springs up and paces as Midhurst reads from Swinburne's
Ode to Mazzini:

MIDHURST

"Too long the world has waited. Day by day
The noiseless feet of murder pass and stain
Palace and prison, street and loveliest plain,
And the slow life of freedom bleeds away."

REDGIE

If my verse can serve patriots —

MIDHURST

To bring in the red republic, better to
enroll a score of horrid *picciotti* and set out
at their head.
    (folds up the pages)
I saw the Radworths the other day. Ernest
looks fifty. Clara looks older too. In a year
or two she will cease to be dangerous even
for boys.

REDGIE

The best part of one comes out in flower at
the sight of her eyes. She ennobles any
man she speaks to.

MIDHURST

Then Ernest is indeed a glorified man.

Redgie glares.

MIDHURST [cont'd]

If an acquaintance becomes half deified by
her touch, what must not her husband
have grown into?

REDGIE
The man lacks anything that can respond
to her. Contact with the noblest nature
created only deepens his degradation.

MIDHURST
I see.

REDGIE
It makes the more splendid her endurance
of him, her patience—

MIDHURST
I perceive the point of attraction is
physical: Her good looks (such as they are)
lie at the bottom of this clatter. We women
have our own silly sides, but I am every
day grateful I was not born male. Tea?

INT. MIDHURST'S DRAWING ROOM - DAY

Midhurst sits with Clara. Radworth browses along a shelf
behind them, coming nearer. Evidences of tea.

CLARA
Redgie amuses me, aunt—nothing more.
In a life like mine, one appreciates such a
follower.

MIDHURST
By way of change?

CLARA
I make no complaint.

> MIDHURST

Of course not. Complaint is not a game permitted. The cards would burn your fingers.

> CLARA

The situation is harmless on all sides — even creditable.

> MIDHURST

That makes it the more dangerous. I have a plan for Frank and Redgie to travel together. Frank is unencumbered, I believe?

> CLARA

He has all summer before his studies resume.

> RADWORTH

But my dear: Portsmouth.

Clara flinches.

> MIDHURST

Portsmouth?

> RADWORTH

Our boating holiday.

> MIDHURST

All of you?

> RADWORTH

Oh yes.

CLARA
(rising)
Hadn't I mentioned it? Nothing is certain.

MIDHURST
It sounds a pleasant plan. I know you will upset yourself, but to be sure sentiment can't survive a capsize.

Radworth laughs uncertainly. Clara glares.

INT. MIDHURST'S DRAWING ROOM - DAY

Midhurst sits with Frank. Evidences of tea.

FRANK
Clara keeps him alive. Left to himself, Ernest would never eat, but crunch up a bone right there in his ossuary and go back to work.

MIDHURST
And Amy? Do you see anything of her?

Frank looks faintly surprised.

MIDHURST [cont'd]
They are in town. Edmund is sniffing about the House of Lords. You must call. It is only polite.

FRANK
Of course I will.

> MIDHURST
> You are a refreshment after my insane
> Redgie. No one can drive him as yet, but
> we shall. Kick he will, but his mouth shall
> ache and his flanks bleed for it. I hoped
> you might carry him out of danger to Italy,
> but Portsmouth—

> FRANK
> Oh aunt, in Italy he would enlist us both in
> some doomed volunteer corps. Portsmouth
> will be safer.

> MIDHURST
> Doubtless you are right. I believe in your
> good sense.

They smile at each other.

INT. THE BRITISH MUSEUM - DAY

Radworth and Edmund trudge along a corridor.

> RADWORTH
> I mean to leave my collection to the nation:
> "The Radworth Fossils."

> EDMUND
> A utilitarian thought, sir. I too see hope for
> the people in the British Museum. I agitate
> for evening hours and—

> RADWORTH
> Evening hours?

EDMUND
The working man can come at no other
time, and what these galleries want is the
working man. Evening hours and Sunday
opening will—

Radworth halts.

RADWORTH
Sunday opening? You jest.

EDMUND
It would save the working man from the
stimulants of doctrine!

RADWORTH
Oh dear. The working man.
(Cheers up)
Ah! This gallery will interest you: Horns of
all the beasts of Africa. The most curious
things!

They hurry into a gallery of horns.

INT. MIDHURST'S DRAWING ROOM – DAY

Midhurst sits with Amy. Evidences of tea. Amy begins to cry.

MIDHURST
Things tend towards entanglement like
your eyelashes in the wind.

AMY
How do you mean, *grand-mère?*

MIDHURST
The family complications! You must be
cautious of letting people talk again.

AMY
Talk?

MIDHURST
If any breach begins between your
husband and Frank, help it in a quiet way
to widen. A child would save you— A son,
else Frank is the heir, and *that* wouldn't do.
He mustn't hover about Lidcombe.

AMY
Oh *grand-mère,* when my husband speaks
to me— It's worse not to love him than it
would be to leave him.

MIDHURST
That is nonsense.

EXT. BELGRAVE SQUARE – DAY

Amy leaves Midhurst's house and climbs into her coach.

INT. AMY'S COACH – DAY

Frank sits beside Amy in the coach, its blinds drawn.

FRANK
How was the old griffin?

AMY
Oh Frank: She knows.

He presses his body over hers.

> AMY [cont'd]
We can't.

> FRANK
Tell him Hampton Court.

> AMY
I can't.

> FRANK
Then I will.

She puts her head out and calls to her coachman.

> AMY
Henry: Hampton Court.

> HENRY
Hampton Court, my lady?

> AMY
Hampton Court!

The coach rattles off up the street.

EXT. HYDE PARK – DAY

Clara and Redgie walk through a late spring landscape.

> CLARA
Look, Redgie: Roses.

> REDGIE
It is monstrous to see things as they are
and let them go on. We cannot live and lie.

CLARA

Oh Redgie, I know you're right.

She pauses to sniff at roses. Redgie, not noticing, walks on.

REDGIE

I summon you to break off your hideous compromise. Who could blame you if you left? Who can help blaming you now?

CLARA

Do be kind.

REDGIE

Say why you go, and go at once. Go to Frank. He will exult that you choose him to serve you. As for me— I believe you will let me see you sometimes. I wish I knew how to say that I love you as no man has ever loved.

CLARA

We must go back. They will miss us.

REDGIE
(closing his eyes)
I have the desire for your face that wounded men have for water. We can trifle no longer.

CLARA

No, we cannot.

She places an envelope in his hands. Redgie opens his eyes, radiant, and sniffs the letter.

                    REDGIE
          Darling! Tell me—

                    CLARA
          I cannot say these things.

She walks tragically away. Redgie closes his eyes.

INT. REDGIE'S CLUB – NIGHT

Redgie sprawls in a chair, flanked by elderly sleeping
gentlemen. He smiles at Clara's letter, kisses it, sighs and tears
it open. He reads it, jerks up in his chair, runs out of the room,
colliding with people and objects.

The elderly gentlemen wake up.

                    ELDERLY GENTLEMAN
          The rabble?

                    SECOND ELDERLY GENTLEMAN
          Daresay a woman.

                    ELDERLY GENTLEMAN
          Oh.

They go back to sleep.

INT. MIDHURST'S DRAWING ROOM – NIGHT

Midhurst spreads three letters across her lap. Redgie sits
looking tragic.

MIDHURST
My "anxious and affectionate niece" has
told me all, Redgie — and sent a copy of her
grand renunciation.
    (compares Redgie's copy)
She enjoys her game too much.

REDGIE
Say what you will —

MIDHURST
You *are* fun. I have been laughing for
hours. "I could explain and advise. To her
husband she could not turn for counsel."
Hear the thrilling note of British
matronhood? "Is she to appeal to your
noble nature?" Indeed, you behave nobly.
A fool you may be, but you get through
your fooleries like a gentleman.

REDGIE
Grandmother —

MIDHURST
"I no more mean to leave Ernest because
we might have more in common than I
should have thought of marrying a man
for his title." How kind! And more
padding for the blow: "Forgive me if this
letter hurts you. Of course you can never
show it."

REDGIE
Grandmother —

MIDHURST
That last, faithfully copied to me, lifts this
into genius—of a kind.

REDGIE
I must go.
   (sinks down)
The pain is more than I can bear.

MIDHURST
Redgie Seyton, you have been trained from
a boy to carry pain—trained to the
discipline of circumstances. Look more
closely: Her magnanimous bits are
impertinence! I tell you, she married the
man tooth and nail, as a hawk takes a
rabbit. She cares for duty no more than I
should care for her reputation if she were
not my relative. She is a thoroughly
cautious woman: There is nothing to be
made of Clara.

Tears come into Redgie's eyes.

MIDHURST [cont'd]
Now you hate me, and it's useless to beg
you to stay in town and end your
sufferings sooner than you will at
Portsmouth.
   (rising)
Anyway, stick close to your sister, and
don't sink in Platonic slogs of love:
Sentiment will soak you to the bone.

She embraces him.

EXT. HARBORSIDE, PORTSMOUTH – DUSK

As the June sun sinks, Frank and Amy walk, emitting an electric awareness of each other.

TITLE:

Portsmouth

Amy holds up her hand in front of her.

> AMY
>
> My ring burns.

> FRANK
>
> I don't see why we should alter our plans.

> AMY
>
> Think of your honor. My hand ought to be cut off. I am ashamed of every breath I draw.

> FRANK
>
> I will not plead with you. If you were to die tonight I should still have had more than my share of luck in life.

> AMY
>
> He is so good to me. If I were to die, I should never forget that!

> FRANK
>
> Tongues would wag at any change of plans. What can people say as things are?

AMY
This sense of a secret wears me out. I wish
Edmund would kill me.

FRANK
You might care for me a little more. We
don't want the clack of love—I know you
detest that—but—

AMY
If you love me so much, you ought to be
sorry.

FRANK
I do love you.

AMY
It is too late for me to get happy again.

She holds up her hand. Frank kisses it. They walk on.

EXT. DOCK IN PORTSMOUTH HARBOR – DAY

A brilliant morning. A gleaming racing yacht, manned by three
SAILORS, rides at dockside. Redgie settles Amy and Edmund
in its stern. Radworth and Clara arrive. Clara maintains a frigid
distance from Redgie, whose reproachful glances escape him as
Radworth attends nervously to Clara. She directs him to a place
farther up while she sits with Amy. Frank arrives. He speaks to
Redgie and Edmund.

REDGIE
Do come, Frank, we need you.

EDMUND
Sailing is a cooperative endeavor, Frank,
and having beforehand agreed, I don't see
how —

CLARA
Come on, Frank.

FRANK
Oh all right.

Amy looks reproachfully at Frank.

EXT. ABOARD YACHT OFF PORTSMOUTH – DAY

Helped by Edmund, Redgie handles the sails and directs the
sailors. Radworth holds on to anything steady, uncomfortable
but game. Frank works the tiller, but gives his attention to
Amy, who looks guilty and unwell.

CLARA
The sun and air will revive you, Amy.

Amy gives her a sick look and lies back so as to avoid Frank.

CLARA [cont'd]
Amy? Dear, are you ill? Edmund! Redgie,
tell Edmund — Redgie!

Neither Edmund nor Redgie hears her.

CLARA [cont'd]
Ernest, tell Edmund Amy's ill.

RADWORTH
What?

Radworth rises unsteadily and pitches against Redgie, knocking him over and the boom out of his hands. It swings around and sweeps Edmund overboard.

Redgie jumps in. The others converge on that side. Frank fights for control of the boat. Redgie dives many times before he finds Edmund. Frank gets the boat turned around. The sailors pull in Redgie — gasping and spewing water — and Edmund. They pump Edmund's arms, but he is dead.

Amy grabs Redgie's hands, chafing her face with them and kissing them, stunned.

EXT. DOCK IN PORTSMOUTH HARBOR – DAY

The yacht lands. With a sailor's help Redgie carries Amy up to her hotel. Clara is excited.

> CLARA
> He was splendid.

> RADWORTH
> Who was splendid?

> FRANK
> Redgie was. Cool and brave. If there had
> been a chance —

He shakes his head.

INT. HOTEL SITTING ROOM, PORTSMOUTH – NIGHT

Redgie consoles dry-eyed Amy. Frank and Radworth sit to the side. Clara comes out of a bedroom with an UNDERTAKER. Amy shrinks back.

CLARA
(to Amy)
I'm sure you want to see him.

UNDERTAKER
(to Frank)
A sad business, Lord Cheyne. Very sad
affair, your lordship.

Amy revolves toward Frank, who drops into a chair.

CLARA
Redgie, you were splendid.

Redgie looks ravagedly into her eyes and kisses her hands.
Radworth dabs at his eyes.

EXT. HIGHGATE CEMETERY, LONDON – DAY

Drizzle. Edmund's funeral. The Cheyne Mausoleum stands
amidst a group of little marble temples. Midhurst, Redgie,
Frank, Clara, Radworth are among those in attendance, all in
mourning (which in various degrees they will wear until the
end). Redgie attends to Amy but is aware of Clara; Frank
cannot get near Amy. The only sounds are the tolling of a bell,
the mumbling of a PRIEST and the keening of professional
MOURNERS. Edmund's black coffin is carried in and placed
on its shelf. The pallbearers come out. Amy, dry-eyed, comes
out behind them.

The bronze doors close. Midhurst, upset, leads Amy to a black-
draped coach. They climb into it with Redgie. It moves off at a
stately pace.

INT. MOURNERS' COACH – DAY

Amy stares out a chink in the blinds as the white terraces of Highgate roll past.

> REDGIE
> Grandmother, if I can help clear
> Lidcombe —

> MIDHURST
> Thank you. Yes. I don't know. I'll go up —
> oh, in a few days. I'm sure Frank will give
> us that.

> REDGIE
> He is overcome —

> MIDHURST
> *Shhh.*
>   (envelopes Amy in her arms)
> The change is sharp, child. All changes are
> that turn upon a death. You believe you
> will never get over the pain. But self-
> reproach is an idle thing. Refuse the
> relaxation of complaint and face things as
> they are. Show honor to his memory by
> controlling yourself. Those who cannot
> support themselves cannot be supported. I
> know my counsel is harsh, heathen,
> mundane, but I have lost many people,
> many things I would have given much to
> keep. I have repented and lamented, but
> repentance never did good or undid harm.

>   (fights back tears)
> If faith upholds you, it is an energy natural
> to you — I am not preaching paganism. But
> liberty and courage are better than
> indulging in penitence. The world will
> dispense with us some day — but not while
> we can hold out. There: I have unpacked
> my bag for you. Now I put it away for
> good. Come, Amy.
>   (kisses Amy. Both burst into
>   tears)
> Poor child, I had to talk her into tears.

Redgie leans across and embraces them.

EXT. FORECOURT OF LIDCOMBE – DAY

Midhurst oversees servants bringing Amy's things out of the
house and loading them on wagons.

EXT. GATES OF LIDCOMBE – DAY

GATEKEEPER opens gates to Frank and Clara's coach.

>   GATEKEEPER
> Welcome to Lidcombe, Lord Cheyne.

Frank sits back as though slapped. Clara smiles.

EXT. FORECOURT OF LIDCOMBE – DAY

Midhurst is dispatching loaded wagons when Frank and Clara
drive up. Frank goes to Midhurst, Clara to the GARDENER.

>   MIDHURST
> Well, Frank — or do you prefer "my lord"?

FRANK
How are you, Aunt Helena?

MIDHURST
Early deaths age people who hear of them.

FRANK
And Amy? Can I see her?

MIDHURST
She's not yet well enough—indeed, daily more purplish about the eyes. She has just now a spiritual tendency—past any medicine of mine. The truth is, she's too young to be a widow.

FRANK
She must be again a wife.

MIDHURST
Oh, she can hardly marry again. A pity she will never have a child. A daughter would have done you no harm and left her with one side of life filled up.

FRANK
She is divided from herself. If she were to go mad—

MIDHURST
I had no suspicion of so deep a love on her part. Poor Edmund can hardly have given her as much. I'm glad you've come to Lidcombe, Frank. You will make them a good lord.

FRANK
They throw the title in my face like a slap.

MIDHURST
There must be a network of law business to
get through?

FRANK
Deeds, and over-lookers, and tenants,
and— I see Amy sitting silent, like a
woman forced to look on while someone
else is under torture.

Redgie stalks out of the house. Frank offers his hand, but
Redgie brushes past.

REDGIE
Come, grandmother.

He sees Clara and goes up to her. She ignores him, making
sweeping gestures at the trees as she talks with the gardener.

FRANK
I never liked him so well. That is how I
want to be treated. Give my love to Amy.

MIDHURST
Redgie!

Midhurst enters her coach. Redgie, looking wretched, joins her.
They drive off.

FRANK
I feel this is wrong.

CLARA
The state of the oaks is a disgrace, no one
has thought of them in years. Philanthropy
begins at home, Frank.

Frank enters the house. The staff's bows and curtsies wound
him. Clara follows, sizing up the staff.

INT. AMY'S BEDROOM, ASHTON HILDRED – DAY

Amy lies in bed. Through the window, arid August. Knock at
the door. She does not respond.

MIDHURST (O.S.)
Amy? Child, are you all right?

Midhurst enters and looks down at Amy.

INT. SAME – DAY

A DOCTOR leaves Amy's bedside. Midhurst looks down with
pity, pride and anger. Amy turns to the wall.

INT. DRAWING ROOM AT ASHTON HILDRED – DAY

Amicia, white-haired and faded, sits with Redgie. Midhurst
enters. Wariston, stout and gray, follows.

WARISTON
What does the doctor say?

MIDHURST
Most singular auguries.

Amicia's face lights up and she leaves the room. Redgie laughs.
Wariston kindles with anger.

MIDHURST [cont'd]
Redgie, if, when you go to Blocksham for
fossil season, you find Frank there, say
nothing.

REDGIE
Although a boy would dispossess him?

MIDHURST
Nothing. False alarms in the posthumous
way can never be excused.

She leaves the room. Wariston rounds on Redgie.

WARISTON
Blocksham! You, sir, will not stir! I forbid
you to go anywhere.

REDGIE
Father—

WARISTON
Upon you and your cousin your conduct
draws down remark and reproach.

REDGIE
I will hear nothing against that most
glorious woman.

WARISTON
Silence! From childhood upwards you
have disappointed me. Discipline failed to
work upon you. Pain could not keep you
right. You are contemptible—
    (picks up whip, strikes at every

word as Redgie submits)
Luxurious — selfish — indolent —
passionate — rebellious — insolent —
unmanly — deplorable — unworthy — idle —
unstable — You will not stir.

EXT. SEA BELOW ASHTON HILDRED – DAY

Redgie and Amy, in mourning, her pregnancy obvious, walk apart along the shore. Redgie seems to come to a decision.

EXT. FORECOURT OF BLOCKSHAM – DAY

We see a tall brick Georgian house on a bright fall day.

TITLE:

Blocksham

Redgie leads a horse as Frank approaches him from the lawn, followed at a distance by PHILOMENE, 17, dark and lovely, in turn followed by her mother, ARMANDE DE ROCHELAURIER, a sharp-featured Frenchwoman, 55. The sight of Redgie startles Frank, but he offers his hand.

                    FRANK
          Redgie.

                    REDGIE
          Frank.

                    FRANK
          Amy?

> REDGIE

She's—the same. Frank, these apparitions trailing behind you—?

Frank shrugs and walks on. Clara comes out, her finger in a large book. The De Rochelauriers pause.

> CLARA

You're here.

> REDGIE

I'm here. What are you doing?

> CLARA

Looking out a reference for Ernest: *Prodgers on Pantology*. Redgie, we'll clear the room sacred to spiders for you. May I present Armande De Rochelaurier and her daughter Philomène? My cousin Redgie Seyton.

Redgie bows.

> DE ROCHELAURIER

And how is my dear and very old friend Hèlène?

> REDGIE

You know my grandmother? I say, Clara, let's have her over.

> DE ROCHELAURIER
Above all things delightful.

Eyes swiveling, she follows Philomène, who follows Frank. Clara guides Redgie to a garden bench.

CLARA
I will take a moment's break. Osteology is
a hard mistress.

REDGIE
Monster! Where is he?

CLARA
Upstairs, not feeling well. He—

REDGIE
His symptoms I do not wish to hear.
     (kneels, plunging his face into
      her hands)
Your fingers leave a taste of violets on the
lips. Clara! If there had not been such a
face as yours in the world—

CLARA
Silly boy, get up. Ernest awaits his
footnote.

REDGIE
Your throat is pearl color, with flower
color over that. My horrid grandmother—

CLARA
Stop that: Lady Midhurst is good to you.

REDGIE
She presumes on her power. She says
things about you—

CLARA

All that makes me sorry is that her habit of laughter shrinks up the heart. Her sardonic patience sits with folded hands and hooded eyes, contemptuous of those who choose either good or bad.

REDGIE

My father is against us, too.

CLARA

You should honor Lord Wariston—

REDGIE

Him? Want proof you're a fool? You're beaten, all's said. Liberty? Cheese for your bread. The smoke of the martyr's bonfire is the refutation of the martyr—in the nostrils of a pig.

CLARA

Get up, silly.

REDGIE

I do like admiring. It is so perfectly pleasant. *Je t'aime. Aime-moi.*

Clara blows dust from her book at Redgie's face. He opens his eyes with a smile of delight.

REDGIE [cont'd]
Merci. Merci. I am so happy.

Radworth appears at a window.

                    RADWORTH
Clara!

                     REDGIE
Ernest is calling.

                    RADWORTH
Clara!

Grimacing, Clara gets up and goes toward the house.

EXT. FORECOURT, BLOCKSHAM – DAY

Midhurst descends from a coach into De Rochelaurier's arms.

                 DE ROCHELAURIER
Hèlène! At your age still traveling!

                    MIDHURST
Armande! I wouldn't miss you for the
world!

They kiss the air.

INT. DOORS, BLOCKSHAM'S MUSEUM ROOM – DAY

Clara opens the double doors.

                     CLARA
Ernest is thrilled. His museum's his life,
but no one ever asks to see it.

INT. BLOCKSHAM'S MUSEUM ROOM – DAY

Clara brings Midhurst, De Rochelaurier, Philomène, Frank and
Redgie into a noble room crammed with tables and cases of
fossil, bone, insect and rock specimens.

CLARA

Ernest?

Radworth stands up behind a skeleton of a two-headed calf.

RADWORTH

Already? Delighted.

His visitors disperse, gawking. Radworth wipes his hands, arranges his spectacles and picks up a bone.

RADWORTH [cont'd]

You find me working on bones of *Hyaena spelaea,* which we found with *Bos primigeins* in—you will scarcely credit!—a deposit containing also *Coscinopora globularis.*

Philomène touches the skeleton.

RADWORTH [cont'd]

I say, please don't touch—

The skeleton crashes to the floor. Radworth hands his bone to Philomène and bends to the rescue.

PHILOMENE

Pour potage?

She puts down the bone and, guided by her mother, stalks Redgie. Frank, amused, steps up to take the brunt of Radworth's tour. Putting her head next to Redgie's over a case of pinned spiders, Clara points to a black widow.

CLARA

Don't you love her hair, the purple of a heartsease?

REDGIE
Features too like a little cat's for me.

CLARA
I suppose she could scratch if *maman* says
to. She means to marry her to Frank.

REDGIE
C'est possible?

CLARA
Or you would do in a pinch.

Redgie moves to a window as Midhurst gravitates towards
Clara.

RADWORTH
—with sepula-like markings, from a
stratum below the ochreous drift sand.
And in the same hyena's cave: *Elephas
antiquus*. So you will agree—

MIDHURST
Hyena's cave? Perfect. Certainly no wolf's
den.

CLARA
From your account of Amy, I'm surprised
you would leave her.

MIDHURST
One cannot live in gloom perpetual. And I
had to see for myself.

(nods at De Rochelaurier)
I have the idea she's been dragging poor
Philomène around for years.

CLARA
She's just seventeen.

MIDHURST
Madame always drags someone. A few
years ago it was that young M. Piccard you
got so fond of. You must remember.

Clara's face hardens.

MIDHURST [cont'd]
Armande, where is M. Piccard? Isn't he of
your party this time?

DE ROCHELAURIER
(to Clara)
You must be so proud of your husband.
Some men collect pictures or jewels.

She passes on, bringing Philomène to Redgie at his window.

MIDHURST
She thinks herself one of Balzac's women—
gets up affairs to order. Amusing to find
her taking up with Redgie.

CLARA
Is it?

MIDHURST
She must doubt Frank. Redgie: Now that
could be a match. I mean with the

daughter. He has a boy's weakness for women twice his age, but surely—?

CLARA

I don't think they'd suit.

MIDHURST

Maybe Redgie *had* better take the mother. But I doubt her politics: Armande always was a legitimist. Curious for her.

RADWORTH

—the diluvial theory as thus interpreted I hold to be inadmissible.

He hands a bottle in which something is preserved to De Rochelaurier. She screams, puts the bottle down, collects Philomène and goes out, muttering *"grotesque, grotesque."* Redgie and Frank follow.

MIDHURST

Clara, Frank should be at Lidcombe, his own seat. It looks poorly for him to be away his first autumn.

CLARA

But—

MIDHURST

If there is anything in this Philomène business, it will grow the better for a separation. But if it's mere motherly intrigue, better to cut loose at once.

CLARA

What are we to do with Redgie if Frank
goes?

MIDHURST

Redgie enjoys the shooting at Lidcombe.
He is unhappy here.

CLARA

He makes himself so.

MIDHURST

I've had enough of this charnel house.

They go out. Radworth stands up, waving a bone. He is alone.

RADWORTH

Here: The socket of an elephant's tusk. If
you require proof as to the coexistence of
man and the extinct pachyderms— Hello?
Hello?

INT. DRAWING ROOM, BLOCKSHAM - NIGHT

Radworth reads. Clara and Frank sit near by. Redgie sits beside
Philomène, who leafs through archaeological plates. De
Rochelaurier knits next to Midhurst.

PHILOMENE
(tapping a plate disgustedly)
Again *les carcasses*. All over this house.

Redgie says nothing. De Rochelaurier shakes her head.

DE ROCHELAURIER
No. I had hoped— Philomène will make a
wondrous wife. But no.

MIDHURST
She seems very tractable.

DE ROCHELAURIER
Redgie waste away. From love? What if he
waste away till he go out—*poof?*

MIDHURST
You can help.

DE ROCHELAURIER
I? How on this earth?

MIDHURST
You possess the sovereign remedy for a
boy's love sickness.

DE ROCHELAURIER
My Philomène he does not notice.

MIDHURST
I mean the letters I heard of several years
ago.

DE ROCHELAURIER
Letters?

MIDHURST
Letters chronicling the attachment of a
young married woman to your M. Piccard.

DE ROCHELAURIER
I recall some letters. Full of "never — ever —
always." *Très belle*. Is it Clara again? Such
affectionate nature.

MIDHURST
Such determination.

Redgie goes up to Clara and speaks in low tones. Radworth,
looking up, adjusts his spectacles. Philomène closes the
portfolio and stares at the fire.

DE ROCHELAURIER
He should be more man of the world.

MIDHURST
He's just starting out. Clara has served for
his first love. To see how she expressed
herself to another man would harden his
sentimental cuticle enough for him to face
life.

DE ROCHELAURIER
You take such trouble for your children.
They are fortunate.
    (puts her knitting away)
Perhaps we come to arrangement.

MIDHURST
Good.

DE ROCHELAURIER
Five hundred?

Midhurst closes her eyes in pain, but manages an affirmative
twitch of her fingers.

DE ROCHELAURIER [cont'd]
We go tomorrow, I think.

MIDHURST
So soon? What a shame!

EXT. SHOOTING GROUNDS AT LIDCOMBE – DUSK

Frank and Redgie, attended by gamekeepers, shoot as the light goes. The house's façade is at rear.

GAMEKEEPER
My lord, it's getting dark.

FRANK
They tell me you may marry Philomène.

Shoots.

REDGIE
They tell me the same thing about you.

Shoots.

FRANK
Watchful as is *maman,* you'd think she could see —

REDGIE
Her eyes turn on springs in her head without appearing to look.

FRANK
When I look at Philomène, there gets up between us a face ten times more beautiful: Pale when I saw it last, drawn down by its

hair, weighted about the eyes with a presage of tears, sealed with sorrow.
          (shoots)
I want my life and my love back. I hope Lady Midhurst may be brought to marry me to the one woman faultlessly fit for me—

                    REDGIE
I don't see that it depends on my grandmother.

Shoots.

                    FRANK
But it does. She has the passion of intrigue and management still strong—likes nothing so well as making and breaking matches.

Shoots.

                    REDGIE
Hardly fair, Frank.

Shoots.

                    FRANK
Your idolatry becomes a bore, Redgie. I wish we could draw your worship off Clara.

                    REDGIE
Your tone—

                    FRANK
Don't you see how you make Ernest
flinch?

                    REDGIE
I have hold of her, Frank. I won't let go of
her for any man.

Both shoot, nearly hitting a beater.

                  GAMEKEEPER
My lord! The light—

                    FRANK
All right, Hitchens.

They begin to walk back.

INT. REDGIE'S BEDROOM, ASHTON HILDRED – DAY

Amy is swollen, Redgie emaciated.

                     AMY
I told *grand-mère* I would tell you.

                    REDGIE
Tell me what?

                     AMY
Oh Redgie, don't let Clara take you away
from us. You know how much we love
you.

                    REDGIE
You aren't well, Amy. Don't let's—

AMY

You talk of Clara's noble nature. If she has any mercy, let her save you.

REDGIE

Do not ask me to forbear loving for others' sake.

AMY

If you knew my misery! False in every word and thought I had. I should like to beat myself. I want to be done harm to.

REDGIE

You repent a laughable baby-ghost of a flirtation—

AMY

I hate repeating what was said viciously.

REDGIE

I know where such hints come from.

AMY

It's no unkindness of *grandmère*'s. Your friend Madame De Rochelaurier writes things about Clara and M. Piccard. There are letters, Redgie, the cleverest she ever saw, but not good to write.

REDGIE

Show me letters to prove I don't love Clara, and I will read them.

INT. AMY'S BEDROOM, ASHTON HILDRED – DAWN

The doctor, Amicia, Midhurst and servants attend Amy as she gives birth. Suddenly an infant cries out. We see Amy's newborn baby boy, and also her joy and satisfaction.

INT. DRAWING ROOM, ASHTON HILDRED – DAWN

Amicia waits. Wariston pets his dogs. Sound of a baby crying. Midhurst enters laughing and pulls on gloves.

> MIDHURST
> I a great-grandmother—and not 63 till next month! A boy: The new Lord Cheyne. Fat and foolish, red and ridiculous. I'm going to Lidcombe, to let them all know.

Amicia and Wariston go out.

EXT. ROAD NEAR LIDCOMBE – DAY

A winter's day. Redgie and Clara ride, Clara employing her whip more on Redgie than on her horse. Redgie looks wretched.

A coach rumbles past.

> CLARA
> Redgie, it's your grandmother!

They trot after the coach.

EXT. FORECOURT, LIDCOMBE – DAY

Midhurst enters the house.

INT. LONG GALLERY, LIDCOMBE – DAY

Frank, Redgie, Clara and Radworth follow Midhurst in.

> MIDHURST
> Forgive me for being abrupt, but we could
> never write. Eight months of mourning
> made us so anxious —

> FRANK
> Aunt, you do not make yourself clear.

> MIDHURST
> Amy has just enriched the nation by a
> child — male.

> RADWORTH
> A miracle! Edmund lives on! Thank
> God . . .! Oh Frank, it's hard on you —

Clara kicks him.

> MIDHURST
> She seemed frail, and a daughter would
> mean nothing here, so we kept our
> counsel.

> FRANK
> How is Amy?

> MIDHURST
> Glittering at sight of the child as if it were
> the sun and she water in the light of it.

> CLARA
> How lyrical.

MIDHURST
Clara, I should implore you to be
godmother if they had not tricked me into
promising. Now, if the men will let us
alone for a moment.

CLARA
Why?

MIDHURST
(to the men)
Shoo! You are not wanted!

Frank, Redgie and Radworth go out. Clara smiles nervously as
Midhurst sits down.

MIDHURST [cont'd]
Here is my plan of action. If you have a
better, please let me know. My old friend
Armande De Rochelaurier got — I have no
idea how — some letters out of the hands of
M. Piccard and put them into mine. Any of
them — your sentiment come down to ink
on paper — would fall on Redgie like ice
and bring him to a sane view of actual
things. I should prefer not to show them —

CLARA
Is there no other way?

MIDHURST
There is assuredly. Write him in a way that
puts an end to his folly for good. Leave no
room for appeal. Say —

CLARA
Thank you, I know what to say.

MIDHURST
Will you say it, is the question?

CLARA
Yes.

Clara moves to a table and writes. Midhurst looks out the window as snow begins to fall.

MIDHURST
As to our year's work, *le dénoûment c'est qu'il n'y pas de dénoûment.* All is as it was a year ago, but for poor Edmund. But the point of such things is just that they come to nothing. Amy and Frank played the game of cousins, and flirting almost warmed to feeling. I enlisted your kindness on Redgie's behalf, and you put up with more than one meant to put on you. No safeguard against liking, is there?

But the time to count up and pay down comes. And the quiet end of friendship is sadder than the stormiest end of a love affair. But we must let things pass: When their time is come for going, we must help them to be gone, and then we had best forget. I wish to see Frank before I go.

Clara rings.

MIDHURST [cont'd]
For my part it's only the canon of the
Church about men's grandmothers that
keeps me on safe Platonic terms—

A servant enters.

CLARA
Ask Lord Cheyne— Ask *Mr.* Cheyne to
step in.

The servant withdraws.

MIDHURST
Someday I shall write a realistic novel on
that topic. The venerable grandmother sees
the hero's ardor cool after an interval of
pleasure, passes him on to his aunt,
seduces the aunt's husband so as to leave
the coast clear, then takes arsenic. I see my
natural profession now.

Frank enters. Clara reads her letter over.

MIDHURST [cont'd]
Mention that I will take him home with
me.

Clara adds a line. Frank sits down.

MIDHURST [cont'd]
Frank, take the time you need to clear out.

FRANK
I leave Lidcombe tomorrow, Lady
Midhurst. I hope Amy will get all right the
sooner for being back here. It is her home.

MIDHURST
You are generous.

FRANK
If all goes well with her, nothing can go far
wrong with me. I shall do well enough for
one of the professions yet.

MIDHURST
The only person who may have any
complaints is —

FRANK
Is — ?

MIDHURST (low)
Ernest. She will punish him for her failure.
I could cry when I think of the thorns in his
pillow, the ratsbane in his porridge.

Clara shows her letter to Frank, who reads it, looks at her and
rings. Clara looks out at the falling snow.

MIDHURST [cont'd]
Very good.

FRANK
It is very good. If Clara ever finds home
too comfortless to put up with, I could not
wonder. And if any man living makes base
use of her innocence —

A servant enters. Frank hands him the letter.

FRANK [cont'd]
Take this to Mr. Seyton.

SERVANT
Yes, my lor— Yes, your lordsh— Yes, sir.

He backs out in confusion.

FRANK
Is it true he is to marry Philomène de
Rochelaurier?

MIDHURST
(she laughs, rising)
No. Do you want her? We owe you
something. I did think of making you chief
manager of the estates, but it wouldn't do.
If the child had been a girl, I meant to
marry you to Amy. But you must forgive
me: The dispossessed lord's marrying the
dowager *would* make the world open its
eyes and lips. Things are better as they are.
Send Redgie to me in my coach.

At the door she passes Radworth, who holds bones in either
hand, trying in utter bewilderment to fit them together.

INT. MIDHURST'S COACH – DUSK

Midhurst and Redgie look out at falling snow.

MIDHURST
I don't ask what she said. I read dismissal
all over you. But you have perfect
command of yourself.

REDGIE

A poor possession. She tells me what she
chooses to tell, and that I am bound to
take.

MIDHURST

Evidently she changed her mind about
several things.

REDGIE

I can't take it out of her for changing her
mind. The best I can do is not get in her
way. My father—

MIDHURST

Come, come: You are not friends, I know,
but your peace must hold. To this day I
don't know why I let him marry your
mother. Redgie, I'm glad your folly about
Clara got knocked on the head. I believe
she's taken to painting already. It would
not surprise me if now she took some
devotional drug. Foreign missions might
be about her mark.

REDGIE
(closing his eyes)
I will hear nothing against her. We shall
always be— friends. I sit here feeling. . .
(long pause)
a breakage inside me.

Rubbing a window clear of fog, Midhurst primps her hair in
her reflection.

> MIDHURST
> If ever she takes a real lover now he will be
> a fool with nice features: That is Platonic
> retribution, the Nemesis of sentimental
> talent. *I* was never in love but once — with
> Prince Metternich, whom I never set eyes
> on in my life.
> > (taps Redgie's knee)
> Come, Redgie, strike her banner. You shall
> hoist a new one soon. I shall marry you to
> a Queen of Sheba yet.

EXT. FORECOURT, ASHTON HILDRED – NIGHT

The coach crunches through snow. We hear a baby crying.
Midhurst gets out. Redgie does not.

> MIDHURST
> Come on, Redgie, don't you hear Lord
> Cheyne calling us?
> > (calling)
> I'm coming, my darling! Coming, my wee
> darling!

She goes into the house.

FADE OUT

Afterword

The Midhurst Lashes conflates and adapts as a screenplay Algernon Charles Swinburne's two novels *Love's Cross-Currents* and *Lesbia Brandon*. *Lesbia Brandon* (which supplies much of the screenplay's 1849 section) is a weird fragment, but *Love's Cross-Currents* may be the best unreadable novel in the English language.

It first appeared pseudonymously as *A Year's Letters* in *The Tatler* in 1877, 15 years or so after Swinburne wrote both novels. Save for some underground notoriety, it failed to garner much attention—the peril, perhaps, of publishing it under the name "Mrs. Horace Manners." In 1905 it came out in book form under Swinburne's name, retitled—not by him—*Love's Cross-Currents: A Year's Letters.*

Both books—saturated with feeling (however perversely expressed), partly autobiographical, partly derived from De Sade and from Laclos' *Les Liaisons Dangereuses*, supremely subtle (and yet operatic)—are dominated by one of Victorian literature's great characters: Helena, Lady Midhurst.

The structure of *Love's Cross-Currents* appears to be transparent: a prologue followed by letters written by members of an extended family recounting their interactions over one year's time. But the text is incomparably dense. Swinburne assumes his multiple voices with wonderful humor, but writes obliquely and obscurely, making no concessions to the reader. Anyone who gets through the book does so only by dint of drawing up a family tree to keep straight its three sets of cousins *(see p. iv)*.

The novel's surface is so impenetrable that it's startling to find beneath it a familiar marriage plot, the family title as the prize: In the course of the year, Midhurst's nephew, Lord Cheyne, dies; her other nephew comes into the title, but the first nephew's pregnant widow (Midhurst's granddaughter) happens to give birth to a son, thus disinheriting him who is the mother's lover and baby's father and bringing the title safely to Midhurst's direct line.

But of course the novel's real action takes place inside these events, in a killing zone of hearts. Midhurst ruthlessly whips her daughter, niece, nephews and grandchildren into and out of affairs and marriages. She promotes, then ends—by blackmailing her niece—her grandson Redgie Seyton's first experience of love (Redgie, it would seem, is Swinburne) and banishes her granddaughter's true love. She hurts every cousin, inflicting pain while flattering her own youthfulness and safeguarding her respectability, and crowns her manipulations by securing—at any cost to others—the family title for her own great-grandson.

Yet despite its tragedies, it's funny, too. I think P.G. Wodehouse must have admired the precisely calibrated austerity of Swinburne's comedy. Indeed, I can't but see Bertie Wooster as another burned-out husk seared by experiences like unto Redgie's.

For Midhurst I wrote with Billie Whitelaw in mind, having admired her movies and—thanks to Prof. Miriam Drabkin, my Latin teacher at CCNY—seen her in New York in Beckett's *Rockaby*.

Perhaps the reader's difficulty in getting at the story *The Midhurst Lashes* retells is the index of its meaning to the author. Control, manipulation, pain, powerlessness, surrender, ecstasy and love in a *haut monde* of play, rivalry and score-settling— perhaps only by packing everything into so dense a mass could Swinburne even raise such issues.

Here's where stripping the story down to a screenplay can be useful. Screenplays are deadly to read because they're not meant to be read, nor is this one: It's meant to be embodied by actors in two-hours' projection of dreamy light. But meanwhile it can serve as an abstract or critique of Swinburne's fiction—lay out his characters and themes in a way his prose resists.

I completed *The Midhurst Lashes* in Los Angeles in 1995, sent it over to Creative Artists Agency, and a few days later was gratified to open my door to a messenger bearing the paperwork that made me a client. A savvy Hollywood friend told me so unlikely an occurrence was probably due to CAA's having recently signed Kenneth Branagh and needing "class" projects to present him. Alas, my script had no part for him, though he'd make a ripe John Cheyne today. But CAA was good to me—

helped me to writing "coverage" (I wish I still had my suggestions for *Runaway Bride* to see if any were adopted), and its librarian offered me a research job. (Should I have taken it? I still can't decide.) But of course what an agency wants is material for moneymaking movies and TV shows, and such has never much interested me. Michael Ovitz gave me a sunny smile at the agency's door one day, but soon departed for Disney. My agent left, too, and one morning I opened my door to a messenger returning my submissions, and that was that.

My adaptation is a reduction. Anyone who likes *The Midhurst Lashes* has a treat in store: reading Swinburne's novels.

Steve Meyers
September 2023

www.ingramcontent.com/pod-product-compliance
Lightning Source LLC
Chambersburg PA
CBHW021213130726
47988CB00002B/640